THE
ADOPTION
MYSTIQUE

A Hard-hitting Exposé of the
POWERFUL NEGATIVE SOCIAL STIGMA
that Permeates Child Adoption in the United States

Joanne Wolf Small, M.S.W.

First published by AuthorHouse 9/20/2006

ISBN: 1-4259-6178-9 (sc)
ISBN: 1-4259-6179-7 (dj)

Library of Congress Control Number: 2006908138

This book is printed on acid free paper.

Printed in the United States of America
Bloomington, IN

Grateful acknowledgment to The American Public Human Services Association for permission to print "Discrimination Against the Adoptee," *Public Welfare*, vol. 37, No. 3, and "Working with Adoptive Families," *Public Welfare*, vol. 45, No. 3.

Cover design by George Foster

Acknowledgments

I am indebted to my husband, Victor Hepburn Small, Ph. D., for the patience, support, and critical assistance he devoted to this project.

Very special thanks to Kathryn Lippman Blake and Carl Susinno for years of camaraderie—we are as one beneath the skin.

And to Anne, David, Joe, Judy, Linda, Ron, Rosemary, Terry and Tom, and to all of the adopted persons, adoptive parents, birthparents, family members and friends that have inspired me over the years, and have contributed in ways large and small to the evolution of The Adoption Mystique, thanks. Many are named, quoted and cited in the essays that follow.

To my adoptive parents, Joe and Anne Wolf

who live on in my heart and my mind,

and whose memory I cherish.

Preface

This collection of essays on adoption, comprising a selection of articles and talks written or revised over a period of years, began to materialize as a book about two and a half years ago. The essays look at adoption from a psychosocial or environmental perspective. They outline the history and background of American adoption culture, and explore the hidden but powerful religious, social, and economic factors that affect our image of adoption past and present. The essays are often critical of child welfare's adoption premises, policies, and practices. Adoption is an industry that has largely gained power from the desperation, neediness and powerlessness of the birthparents, infertile couples, and adoptees it serves. Society has invested the industry with an image comparable to that of a sacred cow. Criticism has customarily been taboo. Recent reforms were forced upon the industry by societal shifts. Nonetheless, and despite protestations to the contrary, the undercurrent of negative feelings and attitudes generally accorded the adoptive family as a variant, and adoptive status in particular, remain much the same.

I cite the occasion on which those essays that are revised and re titled were originally presented, and list them in the order they appear in *The Adoption Mystique.* An associate professor and dean of social work, twice awarded Professor of the Year, first reviewed "Psychiatric Problems in Adopted Children." She said, "Joanne, this paper presents many difficult issues ignored by social workers. I would like to see it in the hands of every adoption worker to help them and the adoptive parents they work with." The revised version is now titled, "The Adopted Child: Clinical Issues and Psychosocial Problems in Living."

"Working with Adoptive Families" was derived from a speech I presented to a conference on "Helping Families with Issues Around Adoption," sponsored by the Center for Family Studies and the Family Institute of Chicago, September 1986. It was entitled, "The Adoptee: Clinical and Psychosocial Issues through the Life Cycle." It was published as "Working with Adoptive Families," in *Public Welfare,* the Journal of the American Public Welfare Association, in Summer 1987, vol. 45, No. 3.

"The Task of Telling" was published in the *ATC* (Adoption Therapy Coalition) *Journal,* vol. V, Number 2, Spring 1996.

"Clinical Notes" was presented to the Washington, DC Society of Clinical Social Workers in December 1999. I, as an adopted person was part of a panel of clinical social workers that included a birth parent and adoptive parents. Some panelists wished to present the adopted child as a subject separate from the subject of the adopted adult. I objected. Adopted children grow up to become adopted adults. Their issues are identical, and remain throughout their lives.

"Discrimination Against the Adoptee" was originally presented as testimony to The Model State Adoption Advisory Panel as "The Dark Side of Adoption." It was published in *Public Welfare,* Summer 1979, vol. 37, No. 3.

"About Open Records," was published as, "Open? Records," in *AIS* (Adoptees In Search) *News Notes,* Fall 1997-Winter 1998. "Open Records Maryland Style 1997" was published in *AIS News Notes*, Spring 1997 as "Open? Records Maryland Style—1997."

Bethesda, Maryland. 2003

Contents

The Adopted Child: Clinical Issues and
Psychosocial Problems in Living 29

Working with Adoptive Families 65

The Task of Telling 87

Introduction: My Adoption Odyssey

"Honey, you are our adorable adopted daughter. Be proud of it and very happy because we love you and wanted you so much" (from the preamble to my baby book, written in my mother's longhand). These welcoming words marked the beginning of my adoption odyssey.

Adoption has long had a place in my life. I have been a member of an adoptive family since I was six weeks old. I share this distinction with an estimated five to nine million other Americans. We can only guess at the numbers. There are no reliable statistics. That is important to me since I find much of what is said about adoption is hyped and propagandized. The numbers are often minimized, distorted, misrepresented, and politicized. Take Bill Pierce, former adoption industry lobbyist for the National Council for Adoption (NCFA) and his "teeny, tiny minority" of adoptees searching.

My parents took a democratic approach to our family. It was our understanding that adoption brought us together because my parents needed children and my brother and I needed parents. That awareness gave us a sense of equality. I do not accept the notion that being adopted, like being Jewish or being female should restrict my rights as a citizen. I believe that adopted persons are entitled to full restoration of the rights that were abrogated. To me it is a matter of equality and social justice.

I am grateful to my parents for their patience, courage, openness, honesty, and empathy. Our family had no adoption secrets. A record of the date and story of my homecoming and the significant events of the first four years of my life were available to me at anytime. I was a curious kid. I asked many questions. They told me my birthmother was young. She ran off with someone. Her family annulled the marriage. "What was my name"? "Rebecca, maybe Roberta." "How do you know"? They said they had papers for me in a strong box. I could have them when I was twenty-one.

The birth of my fourth child put me in touch with my heritage in a way not previously realized. This daughter had blue eyes. That meant I had to carry a blue-eyed gene. It was time to explore more fully my family of origin. It took seven months to find my birthmother. It took ten years, however, "divine intervention," and many false starts to complete a search for my birthfather's side of the family.

I enrolled in a Masters Program in clinical social work at Catholic University about the time my fourth child turned eight. My earliest mentor was a clinical social worker with a private practice in family issues. Her insights and empathy benefited me personally and professionally. The event of my search and my entry into graduate school proved to be adventitious. I knew next to nothing about adoption as a social institution, though I had lived it for three decades. I could satisfy course requirements by researching adoption, child welfare and social policy; psychiatric problems in adopted children and psychosocial problems in living; and the application of traditional family theory to adoption. The latter became the basis for a joint presentation made with Barbara Hoagwood, casework work supervisor, Prince George's County, Maryland Department of Social Services at The National Association of Social Workers 1982 Conference. Our abstract began: "Ways are suggested of psychologically preserving and integrating the adopted child's original family with his new family, while maintaining …confidentiality of identity."

Adopted persons and identity formation formed the basis for my dissertation on *A Comparison of Genetic Identity Indicators Between Adopted and Non Adopted Adults*. Forty-seven adopted persons and 78 non-adopted persons responded to a "Family Background Information Questionnaire." The introduction states, "For the adopted person serious difficulties may be raised by the question, 'Who am I' "? My thesis advisor suggested I could try to get it published in a genealogy text. About another paper "Adoption and the Sealed Record," Dean Judah noted, "Joanne, this is a well written paper, but I think you could make it better by taking it a little further." I did.

My activist role with Adoptees in Search (AIS) almost certainly accounted for my appointment by former Secretary of Health, Education and Welfare Joseph Califano to the Model Adoption Legislation and Procedures Advisory Panel in 1978. I considered the fact that I was the lone adopted person on the 17-member panel of lawyers, social workers, public and private sector agency heads, and advocacy groups a prime responsibility. Most were schooled in the belief that adoption is a one-time service to the child. My goal was to educate the panel to the fact that adoption is a lifelong experience, and that adopted children grow up to become adopted adults. Once that fact is accepted, every part of the Model Act would have to be consistent with that concept. It required that I pay especially close attention. Some panelists gently chided me for hair splitting. Still, it was the panel's tendency to revisit over and again the rationalizations of the past, and to wonder why we should not maintain secrecy, confidentiality, and the status quo.

I wrote "The Dark Side of Adoption" out of frustration. I was given time to present it to the panel, and it was entered as testimony. It begins:

> My personal experience as an adoptee was a positive one. In the social setting in which I grew up, I thought it was O.K. to be adopted. In later life I became involved in trying to establish my own identity, and subsequently worked with many others toward that end. We got, and still get a message loud and clear. It is not O.K. to be adopted! (1979, p.1)

Some panelists were invited to write articles for an upcoming edition of *Public Welfare* on the subject "Adoption: Who Has the Right to Know?" My testimony "The Dark Side of Adoption" became the basis for the article I wrote "Discrimination Against The Adoptee," that confronts what I believe to be the bedrock issue facing adopted persons in our culture. A revised version is included in *The Adoption Mystique.*

I came to the panel believing absolutely in the principal that adopted persons must be treated equally to non-adopted persons. Lee Campbell, a birthparent panelist, and founder of Concerned United Birth Parents (CUB) suggested we strategize. It became apparent to me from a single meeting that our goals were disparate. Birthparents were interested in obtaining information about the child they had given up. It was not *their* civil rights that had been abrogated. In the end, the preamble to the Model Act called for fair treatment of all persons to the adoption. Yet, where rights are in conflict and compromise not possible, the principle that adoption is a service for adoptees shall govern.

Fellow panel member Ken Watson asked me if I would talk to Miriam Reitz about making a presentation to a conference on "Helping Families with Issues Around Adoption," sponsored by the Center for Family Studies and The Family Institute of Chicago. My speech was entitled "The Adoptee: Clinical and Psychosocial Issues Through the Life Cycle." It was September of 1986, yet for many the idea that adoption is a life long experience was still new. About a quarter of the way through my speech a fellow stood up and loudly and firmly demanded that Miriam Reitz stop my presentation, all the while continuing to state his objections. Turns out he was a psychologist doing some research funded by The Cradle and Catholic Charities.

Sometime early in the next year I mentioned the presentation to *Public Welfare* editor Bill Detweiler. He asked to see it.

It was published in *Public Welfare* the following summer, titled "Working with Adoptive Families." Barb Holton, " . . . an adoption caseworker . . . . adoptive and birth parent . . . and 12-year member of Families Adopting Children Everywhere (FACE), an adoptive parents association . . . " took exception. In the "Letters" section of *Public Welfare*, Winter 1988 Holton said:

> . . . I found many of her basic assumptions about adoptive families to be way off the mark.

> There is something disturbing about statements that attempt to define all adoptive families. This article, however, indicts the whole group as being dysfunctional and based on negative premises.

> I found the general tone of the article to be angry. Whence comes such bitterness? . . . It must be . . . difficult for Ms. Small to help adoptive families if . . . she approaches this population as . . . having bad dysfunctional qualities.

> Another interesting but incorrect premise . . . is that . . . people who come to adoption do so as the result of infertility and all the loss that this entails. Perhaps this was the case in the distant past, but it is not factual today. At our agency, most applicants have birth children . . . and wish to add to their family through adoption.

> I do not know what population Ms. Small bases her finding on . . . . Adoptive families do not consider the "child's past . . . a deficit the family should try to overcome." We do not "try to hide the problem," especially since we don't see adoption as a problem. I'm sorry that Ms. Small does.

> I resent such stereotyping. Shame on you! (p. 4)

It was on the basis of the *Public Welfare* article "Working with Adoptive Families" that Ann Hartman and Joan Laird invited me to present a workshop with them, "Empowering Post-Adoptive Families" at the 1987 American Orthopsychiatric Association meeting held that year in Washington, DC.

A sub-specialty of my clinical practice includes post adoption counseling with families, individuals, and couples. I offered a variety of short-term groups including "Women and Infertility" and "Adoption Insights" for nearly a decade through what was formerly the Community Psychiatric Clinic. I helped organize Adoptees in Search following a personal search. Through AIS I led 17 years worth of monthly "Coffee and Conversations" open to adopted persons, adoptive and birth parents, adoption professionals and interested others. AIS did require that participants state their status and identify their interests. It was the first time that some adopted persons or birthparents had divulged their status in a public setting. Note, though, that it was in the context of the search workshops—open only to searchers—or parent groups like "Adoption Insights" that many adopted persons and adoptive parents spoke openly for the first time about their feelings and experiences.

I have made presentations about adoption to diverse organizations like The National Genealogical Society and The Child Welfare League of America (CWLA), conducted in-service training for clinicians, and adoption workers, provided clinical supervision, and published adoption articles in professional journals. All told, I figure I have interviewed about a thousand adoptive family members over a 20-year period.

I believe that most adopted persons prefer to remain closeted, and that is no surprise to me. Though I grew up with positive feelings about adoption I came to realize that others judge adoption—adoptive families—and adoptive status differently, and that remains a personal and professional source of shock, offense, and distress to me. What is more I came to understand that the rules about adoption are a complicated affair. As I presented papers, conducted workshops, seminars and in service training, taught classes, led groups and granted interviews I was exposed to indications of antipathy, hostility, disapproval, mistrust and suspicion apropos adopted persons in our society. Sometimes the silence, denial, and ignorance brought me up short. It was as though there are certain areas adopted persons ought not to go. Since I treated adoption matters openly, directly, and without shame, I had, apparently unwittingly transgressed adoption mores and the cultural taboos surrounding adoption.

Sometimes I have been pleasantly surprised. An adoptive mom told me, "I know why adoptees are searching. I was not adopted myself. But when my parents died suddenly within a few months of each other, I realized the primary sources I had always counted on for family history were gone from my life. I took them for granted—they were always there. All at once I was hit with a tremendous urge to know all manner of things about them, me, my relatives and my history."

I would like to share a couple of other adoption moments. A group of us had gathered in the Maryland state house to testify for open record legislation. Linda wanted to sound out the head of a large private DC agency there to testify against our bill. "So what do you think of the bill, Ms. X"? Linda asked. Ms. X responded, "I think there are just some things you (adoptees) will have to learn to accept in life." "Well that may be true," said Linda, "but let me assure you this is not one of them"! Seems to me that adoption reform could use more Lindas.

I sense many folks find it politically incorrect to use the "b" word in relation to adoption. Yet, I would argue that to own it is to neutralize it. Moreover, there are some of us who can laugh about it. We were mulling over ways other than meetings and search workshops to bring our group of adoption activists together. The holidays were approaching. Carl proposed we have a holiday dance. "We could even call it AIS's first annual 'Bastard's Bounce' "! Carl left us howling and rolling off our chairs.

There is a sizeable body of literature on adoption that includes how to books, personal accounts, and clinical, academic, and research reports. In the early seventies, I went to the library for a book on adoption. Jean Paton's 1954 pioneering book *The Adopted Break Silence* sat alone on the shelf. Since, other adopted persons that have broken silence include Anderson, Fisher, Lifton, Livingston, Saffian, and Strauss.

I tell people I am writing about adoption. They hear babies or children. They think China, Russia, or some other country. They tell me they have a three-year-old adopted child. I try again. "I'm writing about adoption's aftermath—about what happens after the adoption." That does not seem to be worthy of attention or thought when the interest lies in process and a belief that the rest will follow happily ever after. Yet, I find that there is an unmet hunger to understand adoption. I hear it directly from my colleagues, clinicians from other disciplines, adoptive parents, and adopted persons, their spouses and their children. Industry propaganda, third party research studies, and theories fail to tell us the whole story. Perhaps what folks recognize is a disconnect between the institutional image of adoption as portrayed, and their sense of what may be real and what may be important about the adoption experience.

Much of what has been written and said about adoption—the definitions, myths, interpretations and so on—was generated by non-adopted persons, and often without benefit of adopted person's input. No wonder we know so little about adoption's aftermath. That adoption holds sway over millions of people is testimony to the power of its effect. The issues have lain buried, and most of the affected have kept silent beneath the weight of adoption's power. The framework that surrounds adoption law, policies and practice, the beliefs, myths and attitudes that endow it with enhanced and profound meaning, value, and mystery are what I call *the adoption mystique.*

In the fable The Emperor's New Clothes able weavers make very special cloth from special thread they spin themselves from a process they bring forth that is quite secret. The Emperor gives the weavers all things they need to succeed. When the Emperor inspects the goings on, he is assured that the weavers are using extraordinary thread that is very distinctive but only people that are worthy can see it. The weavers challenge the King. "Surely you see it, do you not"? "Oh yes, certainly I do," says the King, not wanting to appear unworthy. Of course, the more he looked the more he imagined he could see what the weavers said they had woven. So the King told everyone that the weavers were very gifted to be able to weave such incredible cloth. In time, people went to see for themselves and as nobody wanted to appear unworthy, nobody wanted to admit what they saw. Indeed the King decreed that the cloth had the ability to tell if people were worthy, and viewing the cloth became a necessary prerequisite to holding office. This assured that a steady parade of cabinet members and court officials visited the weavers and complimented them on their work. The weavers assured the King that, "this is very special work that we are doing for you. It is positively unique"! Finally, when the King tried on his new clothes the weavers exclaimed, "Behold, you look decidedly transformed. Without fail, your court will notice the difference in your highness." The King asked his court, "So how do I appear"? Everybody gave him the highest compliments. "Then I shall parade down Main Street." So he did. The crowd murmured their approval, not one subject wanting to appear unworthy. But a child blurts out with wonder and surprise, "Mommy, why is the King wearing no clothes"? The strong willed child was not going to be put down. The crowd, as if breaking from a trance, realized all at once. "The child is right"! That made a deep impression on the King, for it seemed to him that they were right. Still, he could not admit to that. So he marched on. And the chamberlains walked with great dignity, carrying the train that did not exist.

My odyssey continues . . .

American Adoption: A Shame-Based Culture

Like most Americans, Boston Globe columnist and Pulitzer Prize nominee Adam Pertman (2000) and his wife knew next to nothing about adoption. In retrospect, what they thought they understood was erroneous, distorted, and misguided (p. x). As were the opinions they formed (p. x). The Pertman's experience is neither unexpected nor uncommon. It is testimony to the power of American adoption culture.

Procedures for adopting children in the United States produce an incongruity between the actual and the expected results. Despite social and legal precedents designed to say it is not so, people feel, see, hear, and sense that adoption is different. They find it to be dissimilar in nature, quality, and form. Perhaps that is because adoption is a social convention contrived to artificially imitate and purposefully substitute for what most people consider to be the real thing (Raymond & Dywasuk, 1974; Kadushin, 1974).

The fact that adoption is different is what makes it curious and interesting. Stories about searches and reunions, legislative efforts to open records, and adoptive vs. birth parent custody battles feed the public's appetite and provide grist for the media's mill. A promo for Barbara Walter's annual Academy Award's special features her querying guest Faith Hill, "You searched for your birthmother"? (Geddie, 2001)

1

Discomfort About Adoption

Still, we know little about adoption. People seem uncomfortable getting past the how to adopt to the what of adoption. Moreover, society presumes to shield the affected from their shame. The facts are often sugar coated, censored, or suppressed. Speaking of them publicly sounds too harsh, too angry, or too bitter. Our perception is that information about an adoption is sensitive, secret, and private. We act as though such information carries a risk of exposure to injury or loss. Referring to illegitimate status, "the bad seed" and bastardy is primarily taboo when discussing adoption. Yet, that is core to understanding what being adopted means.

Talking Around Adoption

There are ways to talk around adoption. A local agency sponsored a conference on "Adoption and Child Development." The primary speaker was the chief of psychiatry at Children's Hospital. He began, "I really don't know anything about adoption, but I am happy to talk about child development." During subsequent seminars like "Adopted Children and Learning Disabilities" and "Adopted Children and Attention Deficit Disorders" guest experts similarly began, "I really don't know anything about adoption. But I am happy to be here to talk about . . . "

The Puzzle

The early academic research and literature on adoption is limited. Data is restricted primarily to anecdotal reports from clinicians, social workers, and adoptive parents. Ann Hartman, dean and professor emerita of Smith College School of Social Work said we still lacked enough information about adoption to know the right questions to ask (personal communication, March 1987).

Adoption is a subject shrouded in mystery. Its rules, mores, language, customs, values, and traditions are obscure and hard to comprehend. It is puzzling and difficult to explain. This is true for adoptive parents, their adopted children, their siblings, and the members of their extended adoptive families. It is true for the spouses and offspring of adopted persons. And it is true for adoption professionals, people considering adoption and those without any personal connection to adoption. There are two possible explanations.

First, American adoption practice is rooted in a closed, shame based and paternalistic social system, influenced by shifting and conflicting political, social, moral, religious, and economic factors. These include attitudes toward marriage, procreation, illegitimacy, and single parenthood, and values like privacy and openness, parental rights, the best interests of the child, and a woman's right to choose.

Second, the dominant culture places its highest value on the procreative family. It is the gold standard. By contrast, society perceives adoption as a deficit. Adoption insider and law professor Elizabeth Bartholet (1993) protests adoption's status as " . . . a second best substitute for the biologic child" (p. 31), and objects to " . . . the fact that society weighs in to make adoption the last resort" (p. 24). Adoption insider and sociologist H. David Kirk (1988) finds:

3

> . . . The overt, verbally expressed, attitudes toward
> adoption in our society tend toward full and unqualified
> acceptance of this family variant. However, there are
> covertly maintained and expressed value patterns which
> operate against this acceptance and which tend to make the
> adoptive family a deviant type (p. 9).

Talk show host Larry King (2000) asks adoptive parent Connie Chung, "What is it like . . . what is it like, the feeling of adoption"? King's observations reflect the dominant culture's widespread discomfort with, mistrust of, and disbelief that a family structure devoid of blood ties is equivalent to a procreative family.

Nurture vs. Nature

At one time America treated child adoptions with less secrecy and more openness. The original birth record and the adoption records were not generally placed under seal. The Massachusetts adoption statute of 1851 was intended primarily to " . . . provide evidence of the legal transfer of a child by the biological parents to the adopting parents and provision for a public record of the transfer" (Kadushin, 1974, p. 559). The statute became a model for many state adoption laws (p. 521).

But social ideas like nurture versus nature and the melting pot theory portended change. They fostered a belief that in the adoption of children environment superseded nature. This certainty in the supremacy of nurture over nature led to the creation of a fundamental adoption fantasy—that in the adoption of a child his or her ancestry could be denied, hereditary influences nullified, and illegitimate status theoretically obscured. Thus, adoptive family influence achieved primary importance. Adoption policy embraced the fantasy and moved to protect it. To eliminate the shame factor adoption practice shifted toward secrecy and a closed adoption system.

State legislatures across the country began to seal birth and adoption records. The practice applies to all adoptions—relative and non-relative—in the United States. "A corollary of these laws has been the adoptive parent's feelings that birth parents should cease to exist once the child has been relinquished and legally adopted by others" (Baran, Pannor, & Sorosky, 1974, p. 531).

A new American adoption culture began to evolve in the late 1930's, rooted in unique beliefs consistent with current social values and theory. It spawned several fresh, powerful and enduring myths designed to compensate for, counter and offset reality. "You grew in my heart, not under it." "She loved you so much she gave you up." And the story of *The Chosen Baby* (Wasson, 1939). All fit the predominant bias that, " . . . A child who is given sufficient assurance of love will not need to know about his heritage," says insider and author B. J. Lifton (1979, p. 21). But the myths foster apologies, euphemisms and rationalizations that are romanticized, fantasized and self-serving, and ultimately impose unrealistic expectations and undue burdens upon adoptive family members.

Whose Rights Prevail?

The needs of birth parents, adoptive parents, and adopted persons relate primarily to their roles. Adopted adults seek to restore a right that was abrogated—direct access to the original and uncensored record of their birth. Birth parents seek to know the child they gave up for adoption. Adoptive

5

parents seek to keep adoption and birth records sealed. They currently find themselves pitted against each other in a culturally contrived conflict over whose needs will be met and whose rights will prevail.

Who is Affected?

The inspiration to characterize adoption as a culture or group formed around common interests, patterned behaviors, learned survival techniques and shared experiences, including collective language, symbols, rules, traditions, values and norms came from an article about clashes over competing values within the deaf community (Arana-Ward, 1997), and other articles on American Deaf Culture. References to adoption insiders include family members that gain understandings of the real nature of adoption from living it, as distinct from those that are not involved in living it.

Adoption may directly affect one out of eight Americans. There are no reliable statistics (Downs, Moore, McFadden, & Costin, 2000), but estimates of adopted persons in the United States, including children and adults, range from five to nine million. The lower bound estimate of five million is approximately 2.5 percent of the total population. For every adopted person count at least one adoptive parent and two birth parents, plus additional siblings, grandparents and other extended kinship.

Antecedents of the American Adoption Culture Today

Until the mid-1800's parentless, poor, and dependent children were placed in orphanages or indentured (Kadushin & Martin, 1988). Later, the primary source of dependent children shifted to the illegitimate and abandoned offspring of America's unwed mothers, and the adoption of infants by infertile, married couples became more commonplace. Though the practice of finalizing adoptions often involved legislatures " . . . passing special acts providing for the adoption of particular children by particular adults" (Kadushin & Martin, 1988, p. 535). Some form of adoption legislation was in place in every state by 1929.

An adoption industry began to emerge in the 1910 to 1920 period. Private agencies began offering services limited specifically to adoption (Kadushin & Martin, 1988). Oftentimes, founders had personal connections. Adoptive parents Richard and Ruth Barker established The Barker Foundation in Washington, DC in 1945. Edna Gladney, of the eponymous Texas agency, and her efforts to remove the word illegitimate from Texas birth records became the subject of the film *Blossoms in the Dust*. Gladney suffered the suicide of a sister, for whom the revelation of the sister's adoptive and illegitimate status proved tragic.

Socially connected and economically secure volunteers staffed many early agencies. Many were motivated by a need to help. Their social work preceded today's professional child welfare workers. They bore direct witness to the problems faced by infertile couples and unwed mothers. Their experience gave adoption a very human face. Their values influenced adoption practice and adoption law (Kadushin & Martin, 1988). The Child Welfare League of America (CWLA) first published standards for adoption agency practice in 1938. These standards are rooted in a common Judeo-Christian tradition. They reflect shared social values regarding marriage and family, and uphold societal attitudes toward monogamy, adultery, and illegitimacy.

The American associationists like Thorndike, Watson, Hull, and Skinner greatly contributed to the environmentalist's influence on adoption policies in the first half of the twentieth century. In a study on adoption practice Schapiro wrote, "Agencies shared the conviction of pediatricians, psychiatrists, and psychologists alike that, in general, environmental influences are of paramount significance in the physical and emotional development of children" (Cominos, 1971, p. 73). Helen Cominos, Child Welfare Supervisor, Lutheran Family and Children's Services in Saint Louis suggests, "Social workers are inclined to adhere to this belief with extreme devotion" (p. 74).

There is no mistaking the intent behind confidential court proceedings and sealed birth and adoption records. It was to cut old parental ties and replace them with new ones. A 1951 state of Mississippi adoption survey advocates a "clean break" between the birth family and child (p. 20). *Philadelphia Medicine* (Pennsylvania Citizens Association, 1953) says, ". . . modern knowledge indicates it [a clean break] is in the best interest of the child itself, and all the other parties to the adoption" (p. 223). Oklahoma's State Department of Public Welfare (1954) advises:

> You want to be certain that your adopted child has no family ties which may threaten you in years to come. It would not be possible for you to feel that your adopted child really belonged to you unless you are assured that the separation has been final and legal.

Further, Louisiana's State Department of Public Welfare (1952) warns, "When the adoption is completed, the child is wholly yours . . . No one can trace him through any official record - even his original birth certificate has been sealed where no one can see it . . . " (p. 18). CWLA director Joseph Reed concurred that protection was best " . . . against interloping or worse by the natural mother" (Kiester, 1974, p. 59). Yet, the complete separation of birth and adoptive parents that is common in American society is not universally the case (Weinstein, 1968).

The Deficit Perspective—the Dark Side

For the better part of the twentieth century white, single daughters of the middle, upper-middle and upper classes were taught that good girls said, "no." Bad girls "put out." Those that were "caught" were thrust into a state of disgrace and disrepute. An out of wedlock pregnancy was a public symbol of a woman's transgression. Her reputation was ruined, her family dishonored, and her offspring illegitimatized. Her "mistake" implied an in your face violation of the rules, and a threat that strongly held social and sexual controls had failed.

The punishment for unwed mothers was the relinquishment of their babies. Consequently, their offspring became indelibly marked irregular, inferior, spurious and of bad seed. It was common knowledge that " . . . the image of the unwed father was always a seedy one. He was a man who skipped town one step ahead of the shotgun. He left behind a woman 'in trouble,' and a child who grew up a swearword" (Goodman, 1979, p. A 15). All but forgotten is the fact that many of these babies were the grandchildren of America's dominant economic and social strata.

The pervasive perception is that placing a child for adoption successfully fulfills the needs of the child, the birthparents, and the adopting parents. All will " . . . simply go on in their way to live 'happily ever after' " (Brodzinsky & Schechter, 1990, p. xi). It is an idyllic melding of problem and solution—a perfect fit. But such symbols, metaphors, and images tell a different story. They unmask the dark side of adoption, and reveal the dominant culture's negative and punitive beliefs and attitudes. Whereat adoption is not in accordance with what is morally right or good. It is not proper or usual. It deviates from accepted and recommended practice (Stein, 1967, p. 1648). The dark side of adoption is ubiquitous, enduring, well ingrained, and seldom questioned. It is a part of the air society breathes. It forms the matrix from which comes the premise that there is something wrong with adoption.

Thus, adoption represents a deficit state. One that is wanting, lacking, or functionally impaired, and in need of reformation, improvement, correction or treatment. People that hold a deficit view see differences in adoptive family structure as deviant or pathological when held against procreative or biological family standards or norms. A deficit or clinical/pathological perspective stresses dissimilarities over similarities. Deviation equates with maladjustment. Adoptive status is associated with psychopathology. Constructs like genealogical bewilderment and the meaning of search connect heredity, ancestry, family history, and lineage with pathology—not genealogy. A deficit perspective is identified with a medical model of adoption.

Historically, psychoanalytic theoreticians and social workers embraced the deficit or clinical/pathological model to understand adoption.

Psychoanalyst Povl Toussieng (1962) suggests that adoptive parent's unresolved resistance to parenthood causes emotional conflicts in their adopted children. Insider and psychologist Eda LeShan (1977) opines that adoptees that search appear to lack impulse control not unlike thieves. Psychoanalyst Luis Feder (1974) describes " . . . an 'adopted child' pathology, which can flower into narcissistic character disorder, psychotic episodes, delinquency, homosexuality, fantasized or attempted suicide, incest, homicide, fratricide, murder of one or both adoptive parents, and to patricide and or matricide" (p. 491).

Psychologist David Kirschner (1998) coins like behaviors the "adopted child syndrome," or ACS (Kirschner & Nagel, 1998). About ACS Harvard law professor Alan Dershowitz (1994) cautions:

> Adopted children of the world beware. A new variation on the abuse-excuse defense is about to stigmatize and demonize you. Your friends and neighbors will soon be looking at you warily, wondering whether you are afflicted with "adopted child syndrome" and thus pose a danger of violence (pp. 77-79).

The deficit perspective continues to influence clinical theory on adoption.

The Psychosocial Perspective—the Enlightened Side

By contrast, an environmental or psychosocial perspective on adoption incorporates influences from the dominant culture and the social environment into an environmental or psychosocial framework. This perspective recognizes the effects of shame on birth parents, adoptive parents and adopted persons as they interact with each other and with the culture's legal, social, and institutional systems, values, and attitudes. The significance of the social milieu on adopted child development, adoptive family structure, adoptive family minority status, the adoptive parent-child bond, parental adjustment to adoption, and infertility, adoption practice, and the extent that society condemns adoption is integral to an environmental or psychosocial model of adoption (Small, 1987).

An environmental or psychosocial perspective is broader, more inclusive, and less recognized than one dominated by psychoanalytic theory. People that hold it see adoption as a positive and viable alternate— representative of multiformity or diversification. Differences in adoptive family structure are acknowledged, yet similarities are stressed over dissimilarities. The stereotypic or stigmatic bias associated with a deficit or clinical/pathological perspective is excluded.

H. David Kirk (1964) pioneered efforts to get at the nub of community attitudes toward adoption. His work, including *Shared Fate*, which researched the relationship between societal attitudes, adoptive parent roles, and adoptive family relationships represents an environmental or psychosocial viewpoint. Insider and editor B. J. Tansey said, "I, as an adopted adult, was looking to understand what had gone on between my parents and myself. *Shared Fate* . . . made sense of what I had experienced as child and young adult" (Kirk, 1988, p. x).

Bartholet (1993) suggests, "Adoption should be understood as an institution that works well for birth parents, for the infertile, and for children

. . . as a positive alternative to the blood-based family form" (p. xxi). Insider and psychiatrist Robert Anderson (1993) agrees. "Taken for what it is, adoption is a valid, vital, durable relationship. Differences exist. Recognize the differences. Perhaps even celebrate the differences" (p. 162).

The Fundamental Myth

Traditionally, infertility and illegitimacy were essential links to American adoption culture (Kirk, 1988). Illegitimate, white infants were surrendered to adoption. Married, infertile white couples adopted. In traditional, non-relative adoptions, no biological connection exists between adoptee and adopter. Law totally and artificially creates the relationship. Non-relative adoptions are distinct from stepfamily or relative adoptions, and outnumber all other forms of adoption in the United States.

Procreative Parenthood Exalted

The dominant culture in our society places an exalted value on biological, reproductive parenthood (Kirk, 1988). Insider Adam Pertman (2000) concurs. "Any biologist will tell you we were built to do it. Every culture glorifies it" (p. 130). Infertile couples find themselves automatically placed in a minority subgroup. Those who choose to adopt manifest an even greater and more public deviation from that value.

Denial of the Artificiality of Adoption

Decades of social policy, politics, and practice conspire to deny the artificiality factor in non-relative adoptions. Adoptive family differences are ignored, minimized, or hidden. To the extent possible the child's heritage is obliterated, ancestry stripped, bloodlines expunged, birth certificates falsified, and birth kinship sealed away. To this end, the frontiers of equivalence are pushed toward fantasy and myth.

American adoption culture is grounded in myth. By definition, myths are falsehoods or objects of imagination fashioned from widely held and uncritically accepted beliefs invented to justify social institutions. The fundamental adoption myth is that there are no differences between adoptive and non-adoptive families (Small, 1987). Hence, adopted persons have no existence before adoption. They are neither conceived, nor born. Therefore, they have no ancestry, no genetic history, and no past. In American adoption culture, some adopted persons will say, "I wasn't born, I was adopted."

The Power of the Myth

The extent to which any member of the adoption community values the myth is a direct function of how well it serves their needs. The effect of the fundamental myth on the development of American adoption culture cannot be underestimated. It has been the sine qua non of the adoption industry for the past sixty years. Yet, as Bartholet (1993) suggests, " . . . by structuring adoption in imitation of biology, the law reinforced the notion that the adoptive family was an inferior family form" (p. 170).

Not until their final court appearance did insider and English professor Ann Loux (1997, a) and her husband realize that the surnames of the three and four year old sisters they were adopting would be obliterated from their original birth certificates—and all their public records. They:

14

. . . hadn't thought about it. But the erasure troubled us. It seemed arrogant to eradicate their mother's name—a deliberate denial of the influence of the past upon the present; a rigid insistence that biology and . . . experience—were immaterial in the face of a new environment (pp. 23 - 24).

To gain insights into American adoption culture some recognition must be given to the limits of artificiality and the boundaries of equivalence—and to the adaptive behaviors deployed to protect and conform to the myth.

The Rules

For Unwed Mothers

Society offered women that bore a child out of wedlock a way to make unacceptable behavior acceptable. They could surrender their illegitimate offspring to adoption. Social workers " . . . fostered the notion that women who surrender an infant for adoption are acting in the bests interests of the child and themselves" (Brodzinsky, 1990, p. 295). They told unwed mothers, "you will forget about your child." "You can get on with your life." "You can make a new life for yourself." "Your baby will have a good home, with two loving parents." These messages reflected two positively held social norms. Putting an illegitimate child up for adoption was good. Keeping the event hidden was good. But the messages devalued a birthmother's competence and diminished her self-esteem. Moreover, by surrendering her baby to adoption she doubly stigmatized her status. Society still asks, "What kind of woman gives her baby away"?

She was not to look back and not to come back. Her removal from the system "exnominated" her (Fiske, as cited in Williams, 1998, p. W19). It left her with no name. Some refer to her merely as "she," or "her," as in, "Do you ever think about her"? "Yes, I often think about her on my birthday." Some refer to her as "mother," meaning the woman that bore and delivered them; "Have you thought about searching for your mother"? Others call her the "real" mother as, "I wonder what your real mother looks like"? Some adoptive parents refer to her as "the woman in whose stomach you grew," or as "that lady," or "the other lady." In law, she is the "biological" or "natural" mother. Many people currently refer to her as a "birthmother."

The presumption that, "She had sinned and suffered, paid dearly, and deserved to be left alone" (Sorosky, Baran, & Pannor, 1978, p. 50) justified her exnomination. Conversely, adoptive parents were assured that they would be protected from her. That she would not or could not find them. The system was closed. Social workers told sociologist H. David Kirk (1981) that an exploration of adoptive parenthood was, " . . . neither possible nor desirable; that adoptive families should not have their privacy disturbed and that they must not be made to feel different from other families in the community" (p. 21).

For Couples Wanting to Adopt

The dominant culture values adoption as the choice of last resort. Most people consider it best to have "one's own." Pertman (2000) says:

> No one who hasn't confronted infertility can fully grasp the raw brutality of being deprived of something so fundamental as the ability to reproduce.
>
> It is as though we are being asked to pay the price of violating a social norm, as though our feelings of shame, embarrassment, or inadequacy aren't penalty enough (p. 130).

Persons that choose to adopt must submit to a home study, an investigation into the most private areas of their lives. Many consider it demeaning, though it is understood the outcome is crucial to the pursuit of their goals. Sorosky, Baran, and Pannor (1978) found people, " . . . were afraid to ask questions expressing their doubts and ambivalent feelings. They presented themselves as ideal parenting material because they so desperately wanted a baby" (p. 75).

Applicants that pass a home study are prejudged certifiably fit to parent. People adopting from an agency with a long waiting list, a prestigious reputation, and many applicant rejections might consider their status enhanced. Still, Hartman, Laird (1990), and Kirk (1964) warn that there is a downside to the "perfect parent" requirement. Adoptive parents may feel a need to prove their success as parents. It may raise the expectation in them that they will be superior to reproductive parents. Moreover, society adjudges that they are always "loving adoptive parents," and tells them, "How wonderful it is of you to adopt." Loux (1997 b) came to realize, " . . . how loath adoptive parents are to admit their failures, and how slow some agencies can be to reveal stories of problem adoptions," but the agencies, " . . . are in the business of recruiting adoptive families" (p. C 1). It follows that when problems arise—the cause must be seen to lie within the child.

For Child Welfare

Belief in the fantasy was so complete and acceptance of the myth so absolute that child welfare decreed adoption to be a one-time service to the child. The child's past was sealed away, a new identity was conferred, no overt links remained between the child's past and future, and the child was released from the stigma of illegitimacy. By terminating the service child welfare left adopted children eternally consigned to childhood, with no basis for a change of status. Once an adopted child—always an adopted child is a pervasive image. Some adopted adults say, "I am an adopted child." Media say, "Adopted Children Want to Open Records." "Should Adopted Children Have the Right to Know"?

For the New Family

High positive value was bestowed on the new family. The child's past, if not fully forgotten, was treated as inconsequential. Adoption social workers encouraged parents to tell the child about their adoption. Parents explained that the child's mother could not keep the child. Nevertheless, she loved the child so much she "gave her child away to be adopted." Mommy and Daddy "couldn't have children of their own" so they adopted a child. Some parents chose not to tell at all. Insider and psychiatrist Gordon Livingston (1992) explains that, " . . . as these differences are experienced by the child, the natural questions that arise are often repressed and denied in the interest of preserving the illusion that adoptive ties are the same as biological ones" (p. 2).

For Adopted Children

Children that asked too many questions were often seen as not having made a happy or healthy adjustment to adoption. This made it appear as though the parents had failed and the adoption had not taken. The situation could be especially threatening to parents that hoped to adopt again. Adoptive parents that acknowledged that they had told the child that he or she was adopted might add, "but he (she) has never asked any questions." It could be a point of pride. If questions persisted, a simple, "We don't know anything, the agency didn't tell us anything," was often suppressive enough to shut down communications. The discussion that follows is between an adoptive parent and child. It was excerpted from an article by adoption researcher Kenneth Kaye (1990).

> Mother: You came home and said, "Mother, do I have two mothers?" And we went through "what is a mother?" We went through all the things a mother does—helping her children, making their clothes, shopping, and so on—and I said, "Okay, how many mothers do you have that do those things for you?" And that was the end of that.
>
> Daughter: I don't even remember.
>
> Mother: You don't remember, so that was the end of that! (p. 132)

These strategies helped adoptive families minimize the fact that the child was not born to the parents.

For the Adoptive Family

In an attempt to live up to the fundamental adoption myth parent and child act as if and as though there is no difference between adoptive and non-adoptive family structure (Small, 1987). Yet implicit in the lie says Bartholet (1993), " . . . is the assumption that the adoptive family is in fact a flawed and inferior family form" (p. 59). Livingston (1992) suggests, "The child then takes on, to some extent, the burden of that infertility, and is expected to assuage whatever sense of incompleteness or inadequacy the parents feel" (p. 2).

Insider and Roman Catholic Priest Thomas F. Brosnan (1996) knew he was adopted by age five, though his parents did not tell him until he was twelve. His family did not talk much about adoption nor acknowledge the mutual loss that adoption brought them. Yet, adoption " . . . with all its cumbersome baggage, was in the air we breathed" (p. 1). We were " . . . victims of a closed adoption system which exerts an extraordinarily powerful hold on all members of the triad" (p. 1). Anderson (1993) concurs. "Making the adoptee responsible for the adoptive parent's emotional stability presents a cruel and unnecessary burden. No one benefits" (p. 159).

For Adopted Persons

It is the adoptee's duty to be grateful, loyal, and beholden. Insider and author B. J. Lifton (1979) says, "The Good Adoptee was placid, obedient, didn't ask too many questions, was sensitive to his [or her] parent's needs to make believe he [or she] wasn't adopted" (p. 54). Following a workshop on adoptive families, a young man tells Ann Hartman (1984), "I hate to disabuse you of your ideas about biological ties . . . but I want you to know that I am adopted and I have absolutely no interest in my 'real' family" (p. 7).

"No adoptee was more the 'good adoptee' than me," says insider and theologian John Sweeley (personal communication, August 16, 2001).

> My head was so far up my a— I didn't know if it was raining or the sun was shining. I was so good I convinced myself I had no feelings about my bio-parents or bio-history. This was my parent's wish, which I respected until I was 47.

Then a health crisis led to Sweeley's decision to search.

> As a consequence my adoptive parents disowned me and did not communicate with me for the last three years of their life. Even with this experience the thought that adoptees should have rights never entered my head.

Adoption Today

All the guests on a recent TV show were adoption insiders. Topics included telling, infertility, searching, and feelings about adoption. "What I told my kid is that she came from the stomach of another woman. But she was really meant to be mine. So I adopted her."

"You actually had one of your own, and then you decided to adopt? What made you do that"? "Well, I really just wanted to have one of my own but I had already gone through three miscarriages. That' s when I decided to adopt."

"When you think about who your real mom is, who do you think of"? "For me, my real mom is the one that wiped my bottom, and cleaned up after me." "Would I do a search now? Well, maybe. I have given a little thought to doing a search for my birthmother. But it's more like something that's way in the background."

"No, I have never really given much thought to searching for my real parents. Oops"! "What I'd really like to know more about is my medical background." "Yeah, that's what I'd like to know more about, too. What I'd really like to see is my medical records"!

Anderson (1993) says, "One can be unaware of the importance of his [or her] adoption. Adoption plays a big role in the life of every adoptee. Start with that assumption" (p. 160). Brosnan (1996) agrees that, " . . . For the adoptee, life is adoption. I think this is true whether an adopted person admits it or not" (p. 4).

Accepting the fact that adoption is everybody's second choice " . . . allows one to appreciate what adoption is" (Anderson, 1993, p. 159). It is not natural, but it is real. And the love between adoptive parents and their children can be equal to that of non-adoptive families. Yet, it " . . . falls apart when people expect it to simulate natural" (p. 162).

American adoption culture embodies a deficit perspective. To counter the deficit its rules, values and language enforce the idea that adoption does not matter and that adoption makes no difference. Patricia Williams (1998) in writing about " . . . the notion of color blindness—the idea that race doesn't matter . . . . " suggests that such ideas represent " . . . an ideological confusion at best, and denial at its very worst" (p. W19). " . . . The move to undo that which clearly and unfortunately matters [as in adoption] just by labeling it that 'which makes no difference' . . . " (p. W19) is dismissive. In American adoption culture family members are " . . . pulled between the clarity of their own experience and the alienating terms in which they must seek social acceptance" (p. W19). American adoption culture coaches the affected " . . . upon pain of punishment not to see a thing," and demands that all must " . . . pretend that nothing's wrong" (p. W19). It is not surprising that a majority of adopted persons remain closeted.

It follows that a deficit perspective would move adoption practice toward paternalism, suppression, and repression, and away from self-determination. But legislation has not removed the shame factor from adoption. Nor has it erased public prejudice toward illegitimacy and adoptive status. Not only are secrecy and silence legacies of shame, they are attributions to the power shame holds over adoption.

References

Anderson, R. (1993). *Second choice.* Chesterfield, MO: Badger Hill Press.

Arana-Ward, M. (1997, May 11). As technology advances, a bitter debate divides the deaf. *The Washington Post,* p. A01.

Baran, A., Pannor, R., & Sorosky, A. D. (1974). Adoptive parents and the sealed record controversy. *Social Casework, 55,* 531-536.

Bartholet, E. (1993). *Family bonds. Adoption & the politics of parenting.* Massachusetts: Houghton Mifflin Company.

Brodzinsky, A. B. (1990). Surrendering an infant for adoption: The birthmother experience. In D. M. Brodzinsky & M. D. Schechter (Eds.), *The psychology of adoption* (pp. 295-315). New York: Oxford University Press.

Brodzinsky, D. M., & Schechter, M. D. (1990). *The psychology of adoption.* New York: Oxford University Press.

Brosnan, T. F. (1996, April 24-27). Strengthening families. *National Maternity and Adoption Conference.* Catholic Charities USA. San Antonio, Texas, pp. 1-11.

Cominos, H. (1971). Minimizing the risks of adoption through knowledge. *Social Work. 73,* 73-79.

Dershowitz, A. M. (1994). *The abuse excuse.* Boston: Little, Brown and Company.

Downs, S. W., Moore, E., McFadden, E. J., & Costin, L. B. (2000). *Child welfare and family services* (6th ed.). Boston: Allyn & Bacon.

Feder, L. (1974). Adoption trauma: Oedipus myth/clinical reality. *International Journal of Psychoanalysis, 55,* 491-493.

References

Geddie, B. (Producer). (2001, March 7). The academy awards edition of the Barbara Walters special [Television broadcast]. New York: *American Broadcasting Company.*

Goodman, E. (1979, February 20). A new look at adoption. *The Washington Post,* p. A 15.

Hartman, A. (1984). *Working with adoptive families beyond placement.* New York: Child Welfare League of America.

Hartman, A., & Laird, J. (1990). Family treatment after adoption. In D. M. Brodzinsky & M. D. Schechter, (Eds.), *The psychology of adoption* (pp. 221-239). New York: Oxford University Press.

Kadushin, A. (1974). *Child welfare services.* (2nd ed.). New York: Macmillan Publishing Company.

Kadushin, A., & Martin, J. A. (1988). *Child welfare services.* (4th ed.). New York: Macmillan Publishing Company.

Kaye, K. (1990). Acknowledgement or rejection of differences? In D. M. Brodzinsky & M. D. Schechter, (Eds.), *The psychology of adoption* (pp. 121-141). New York: Oxford University Press.

Kiester, E., Jr. (1974, August). Should we unlock the adoption files. *Today's Health,* 54-60.

King, L. (2000, March 16). First lady praises adoption; Panel of adoptive mothers discuss their experiences [Television broadcast]. *Larry King Live.* New York: Cable News Network.

Kirk, H. D. (1964). *Shared fate.* New York: The Free Press.

Kirk, H. D. (1981). *Adoptive kinship: A modern institution in need of reform* (Rev. ed.). Toronto: Butterworth.

Kirk, H. D. (1988). *Exploring adoptive family life. The collected papers of H. David Kirk.* Washington, DC, British Columbia, CAN: Ben-Simon Publications.

Kirschner, D., & Nagel, L. S. (1998). Antisocial behavior in adoptees: Patterns and dynamics. *Child and Adolescent Social Work, 5, 4,* 300-314.

LeShan, E. J. (1977, March). Should adoptees search. for their 'real' parents? *Women's Day, 40,* 214, 218.

Lifton, B. J. (1979). *Lost and found.* New York: The Dial Press.

Livingston, G. S. (1992, April). Missing pieces. *A T C Journal, 1,* 7.

Louisiana, State of. (1952). *How to adopt a child in Louisiana.* Department of Public Welfare.

Loux, A. K. (1997a). *The limits of hope.* Charlottesville, VA: University Press of Virginia.

Loux, A. K. (1997b, November 23). The catch that came with our adoption. *The Washington Post,* p. C 1.

Mississippi, State of. (1951, April). *Adoption survey.*

Oklahoma, State of. (1954). *So you want to adopt a child.* Department of Public Welfare.

Pennsylvania Citizens Association for Health and Welfare. (1953, September 16). New adoption law for state. *Philadelphia Medicine.*

Pertman, A. (2000). *Adoption nation. How the adoption revolution is transforming America.* New York: Basic Books.

Raymond, L., & Dywasuk, C. (1974). Adoption and after. New York: Harper & Row, Publishers.

Small, J. W. (1987). Working with adoptive families. *Public* Welfare, *45,* 33-45

Sorosky, A., Baran, A., & Pannor, R. (1975). *The adoption triangle.* New York: Doubleday.

Stein, J. (Ed.). (1967). *The random house dictionary of the English language.* (Unabridged ed.) New York: Random House.

Toussieng, P. W. (1962). Thoughts regarding the etiology of psychological difficulties in adopted children. *Child Welfare, 41,* 59-65.

Wasson, V. P. (1939). *The chosen baby.* New York: Carrick and Evans.

Weinstein, E. (1968). Adoption. In D. L. Sills (Ed.), *International encyclopedia of social sciences* (1st. ed.). London: Macmillan/The Free Press.

Williams, P. J. (1998, March 29). In living black and white; the notion of colorblindness – the idea that race doesn't matter – is an ideological confusion at best. *The Washington Post,* p. W19.

The Adopted Child: Clinical Issues and Psychosocial Problems in Living

Adopted children are treated in the literature as though they come from Mars. People isolate them as beings apart, dissociate their experience from that of non-adoptive children, and emphasize their dissimilarities over their similarities. Society fails to recognize that adoption, like divorce, is a condition extrinsic to the child. Labeling them adopted children, not children of adoption, like children of divorce, suggests otherwise. We have the cart before the horse.

In addition to developmental obstacles, difficulties, and exigencies faced by non-adopted children, adopted children cope with questions, uncertainties, and concerns related to being adopted. Their adoptive status — neither their genes — nor illegitimate birth — singularly renders them different. It alone ensures that being adopted is fundamentally unlike being non-adopted. Yet the relevance, significance, and clarity of what being adopted means remain controversial. It is frequently misinterpreted, pathologized, minimized, or denied.

Authors and researchers over-generalize, fantasize, and misconceptualize it. They try to explain it with hypothetical constructs like "genealogical bewilderment" (Sants, 1964) and "the primal wound" (Verrier, 1993). Then reach unverifiable conclusions like "the meaning of search" (Schechter & Bertocci, 1990). They generate speculative attachments like adoption and learning disabilities, or adoption and attention deficit disorders, then assign adoption as causal of, as in an "adopted child

29

pathology" (Feder, 1974), or an "adopted child syndrome" (Kirschner & Nagel, 1998).

These beliefs reflect the culture's pervasive bias toward reproductive family structure; social casework's historic affinity for psychodynamic theory; and the literature on the intra psychic life of the adopted child, from Florence Clothier (1943) and others. All exert a dominant, prejudiced, and persistent effect on public and professional perceptions of adopted children.

Society places high value on the procreative family. It is the gold standard. By contrast, adoption is the choice of last resort. "This perspective has led all other families, including adoptive families, to be defined at best as substitute and at worst as deviant or deficient" (Hartman & Laird, 1990, p. 221). It follows that the same applies to adopted children.

As a social convention, adoption functions to create " . . . the legal relationship of parent and child when it did not exist naturally" (Wade, 1968, p. 56). An adopted child belongs by birth to one kinship group, but " . . . acquires new kinship ties that are socially defined as equivalent to the congenital ties" (Weinstein, 1968). It is " . . . an artificial situation . . . " that " . . . creates families in an artificial way" (Raymond & Dywasuk, 1974, p. 222). As defined, adoption artificially creates, intimately resembles, and is equivalent to non-adoptive parent-child legal and kinship ties. It is not the same.

American social policy, politics, and child welfare practice conspire to deny the artificiality factor in adoption. The "fundamental adoption myth" (Small, 1987, p. 34) — that there is no difference between procreative and adoptive families — has been the sine qua non of the adoption industry for the past sixty years. The myth functions to compensate for, counter, and offset reality.

Child welfare embraced the myth, and moved to protect it. State legislatures began sealing birth and adoption records that were previously open. "Clean break" legislation, intended to cut old parental ties and replace them with new ones, became the new standard. Yet, the complete separation of birth and adoptive parents that is common in American society is not universally the case (Weinstein, 1968).

That the myth imposes unrealistic expectations and undue burdens upon adoptive parents and children has only recently been granted. A 2000 child welfare text concedes, "Child welfare practice was long in acknowledging that most adoptive families are different from other families . . . " (Downs, Moore, McFadden, & Costin, p. 400). Adoption, a principal substitute care service available to children, is part of child welfare, a special field within the profession of social work.

Brodzinsky and Schechter (1990, p. xi) find our understanding of adoption remains quite limited. Long on theory and speculation, short on empirical reference and cross validation, basic questions remain. What do we know about adoption? What attributes are specific to being adopted?

A Diversity of Perspectives

Paton (1954) said, "Above all, adoption is not a 'substitution' for normal family life. Adoption is a different way of being raised, with many resemblances to normal family living. But there are four parents" (p. 54).

Nonetheless, some people maintain an adoption process that amends the birth certificate, confers a new identity, and seals the records, renders the child indistinguishable from other children in the community. Others contend the child will always be different (McWhinnie, 1967).

In *Shared Fate*, sociologist H. David Kirk (1964) says adoptive parent's "acknowledgement of difference" is paramount to establishing a good adoptive parent child relationship (p. 58). Pediatrician William Carey (1974) warns that ignoring the child's background " . . . may represent an unwholesome denial of the realities of the adoption process" (p. 5). Krugman (1967) proposed "The unique task of the adopted child is to handle the issues raised by living in a parent-child relationship that originated in social rather than biological acts" (p. 19).

McWhinnie (1967) found adoption " . . . a complicated experiment beset with problems for the child and parent, and it is not, as is often assumed, one with no more problems than those potentially inherent in any parent-child relationship" (p. 275). Clothier (1943) believed adoption a hazardous relationship, but far less so than the alternatives. She said, "The removing of the individual from his [her] racial antecedents lies at the core of what is peculiar to the psychology of the adopted child" (pp. 222-230).

Schechter (1960) held adopted children must " . . . cope with the knowledge of the rejection by the original parents, representing a severe narcissistic injury" (p. 23). Sants (1964) postulates that adopted children face genealogical bewilderment. They must somehow establish an identity without knowledge of their biological origins. The American Academy of Pediatrics Committee on Adoptions (1971) concludes determining identity is difficult enough for non-adoptive children; it is more complex for adopted children whose ancestry is unknown.

Bohman and Sigvardsson (1990) say adoption's social and psychological context tends to give adoptive families " . . . a minority status" (p. 94). Thus, they " . . . cope with a special existential situation. This may constitute a considerable stress . . . " (p. 94). Yet, the " . . . long-term prognosis for adopted children is no way worse than for children in the general population, provided the adoptive home is psychologically well prepared for the task of rearing a non-biological child" (p. 104).

Brodzinsky (1990), focused on the relationship of loss and stress to adoption, proposed a stress and coping model of adoption adjustment. He concludes, "Whether . . . the model has integrative and explanatory power, . . . remains to be seen. It is . . . too early to evaluate how well the model 'fits' the data" (p. 24).

Finally, Anderson (1993) says, "Efforts to explain adoptee problems range from biological to philosophical, from ridiculous (unconscious comparisons to bowel movements) to sublime (genealogical bewilderment)"

(p. 144). "Since these explanations tend to be abstract and theoretical, they fail to inspire conviction" (p. 145).

These authors reflect a diversity of perspectives relative to being adopted. They include references to the fact of differences; their implications for adopted child adjustment, their association with mal-adaptations, and recognition that some problems are normal to both adoptive and non-adoptive status.

Maladjustment Among Adopted Children

The incidence of adopted children who develop psychiatric problems is undetermined. Given that there are no reliable statistics of the number of adopted children or adults in the United States (Downs et al., 1994, p. 389), it follows that there is no way to ascertain the prevalence of adopted child maladjustment. Some studies have focused on the frequency of referral of adopted children to guidance clinics, or psychiatric services.

Kadushin (1974) notes that "A recapitulation of studies of adopted children receiving service . . . shows a rate of four percent of non-relative adoptions at such agencies as compared with an estimated rate of one percent of such children in the general population" (p. 603). He concludes, "Despite the overrepresentation of adopted children . . . for whatever explainable reason, the fact of the matter is that relatively few . . . receive treatment for emotional disturbance" (p. 578). The data show " . . . only a small proportion need psychiatric assistance. Overrepresentation of adopted individuals . . . although statistically significant, has little social significance" (Kadushin & Martin, 1988, p. 622).

Fanshall says, "The controversy revolves around the question of whether adoptive children and natural born children have the same odds working for them with respect to the opportunity to develop stable personalities and successful life adjustments" (Kadushin & Martin, 1988, p. 622).

Brinich and Brinich found that 5 % of child patients and 1.6 % of adult patients were adopted among patients in service at Langley Porter Psychiatric Institute over ten years. "The researchers conclude that whereas adoption may serve as a focus for psychopathology in individual cases, adoption itself cannot be seen as psychogenic" (Kadushin & Martin, 1988, p. 622).

A series of Scandinavian studies compares adopted children's problems with problems manifest by their birth and adoptive parents. They support the conclusion that adopted persons are more disposed to genetic than environmental influences. The findings are similar regarding intelligence, alcoholism, and temperament (Kadushin & Martin, 1988, pp. 623-624).

Cadoret (1990) says that a large number of twin and adoptee studies show that ". . .behavior ranging from personality traits and intelligence to psychopathology . . . " including " . . . substance abuse and manic-depressive disease . . . " is genetically based. Formerly " . . . environmental factors have been studied extensively in adoptee adjustment, almost to the exclusion of genetic factors" (p. 28).

Lawton and Gross (1964) found only one objective study where adopted children were significantly more disturbed than the non-adopted control group. They conclude that case studies were most often used to support theoretical formulations and practices relevant to adoption; that there is a need for basic, empirical research to test both theoretical formulations and adoption practices, and that case studies serve a purpose, but lack generalizability, are open to bias, and allow free reign of subjective impressions. " . . . A great deal of information has been gathered in a clinical and subjective sense about (adopted) children's needs and parental motives," yet, " . . . there is a paucity of rigorously compiled objective data . . . " (Lawton & Gross, 1964, p. 636).

Child welfare advocates maintenance of confidentiality of information. Confidentiality rules limit significant research by precluding those outside the child welfare domain from access to data. Early academic research on adopted children is limited primarily to anecdotal reports drawn from the observations of clinicians, adoption social workers, and adoptive parents. Adoptees themselves are rarely, if ever participants. Findings are largely subjective, and influenced by, and in support of the researcher's theoretical biases. The result is a preponderance of analytically oriented speculation about adopted child development, and a paucity of data based on psychosocial or psychobiological theory. Research sociologist H. David Kirk's (1964) *Shared Fate* is an exception.

Studies that compare groups of adoptive with non-adoptive children in psychiatric settings fail to demonstrate a unique relationship between mal-adjustment and being adopted. Nor has any problem been reliably identified as adoption specific. Until appropriate control groups are established,

36

comparing matched groups of adoptive and non-adoptive participants, conclusions about maladaptations and adopted children are suspect.

Psychoanalytic Assertions

Analytic theory exerts a pervasive and persistent influence over our perceptions of the adopted child. The analytic literature is rife with interpretations based on psychosexual theory of child development, and clinical observations. For example, in the literature on adopted children and identity formation Hoopes (1990) finds much that is " . . . theoretically based, with the preponderance of conclusions drawn from the clinical data of writers who have attempted to account for the existence of pathology in their clinical patients" (p. 153).

It provided a fertile field for establishing causal relations between adoption and maladjustment, culminating in Feder's adopted child pathology, and Kirschner and Nagel's adopted child syndrome. Yet, Brinich (1990) says " . . . these [Feder's] outcomes are not the result of adoption per se but a confluence of factors that may or may not include the fact of adoption" (p. 52). Moreover, Brinich avers that there is no necessary connection between adoption and psychopathology (p. 42).

Nevertheless, the literature presents adopted children as apt to suffer narcissistic injury (Schechter, 1960) as they are given away by their birthmothers; as prone to disturbances in early object relations as they are taken away from their birthmothers at or near birth; as having problems resolving oedipal issues as they have two sets of parents, one biological and one nurturing; as subject to prolongation of "family romance fantasies" as one set of parents is revealed and the other hidden; as experiencing genealogical bewilderment as they have near zero ancestral information (Small, 1977), an equivalent kinship, and a new identity; and as having doubts and questions around the meaning of search. A review of the purported problem areas follows.

Disturbances In Early Object Relations

Object relations refer to children's mental state, or mental sense, and their mode of relating to other persons, or to their world. Analytic theorists judge early establishment of a continuous object relationship basic to healthy personality development. Early inadequate or unsatisfactory object relationships portend future psychological difficulties. Adoption is considered inherently traumatic because the infant is taken away from his or her birthmother at or near birth, causing a disturbance that enhances the potential for trauma in the child's future.

Clothier (1943) doubts, "The relationship of the child to its postpartum mother . . . can be replaced by even the best of substitute mothers" (p. 223). But Hoopes (1990) suggests, "Clothier's comment typifies the unscientific formulations found in the literature on which conceptions of adoptees are still based" (p. 150).

Freud first recognized the importance of our earliest relationships and their effect on the course of psychic development. When children are helpless and dependent on others for protection and satisfaction of their basic needs, their mother or mother substitute exercises unique influence over their psychic life (Moore & Fine, 1968). At first, infants are unaware of objects as such. Gradually they learn to distinguish themselves from others, and to develop interest in objects that persist when they are not seeking gratification from them. Sometime during the later part of the first year a continuing object relation develops (Moore & Fine, 1968).

The American Psychoanalytic Association states, "Primitive object relations in contrast to more mature forms of object love, are characterized by a relative inability to maintain the love relationship in the face of frustration and to accept the limitations and separateness of the loved object" (Moore & Fine, 1968, p. 107).

Clothier (1942) cites a group of preschool aged children that, following physical and emotional neglect and rejection, were placed in foster care. Most were born to unwed mothers, but not relinquished for adoption. She found that they demonstrated warped and inhibited social, intellectual and emotional development. She said:

> In general, it seems to be true that the child whose psychosexual development has been frequently interrupted by changes of environment that have limited his capacity for identification with love objects is unlikely to be able to form the emotional relationships necessary for healthy social development. These children do not easily make the transition from an orientation toward their aggressive demands to an orientation toward tender, loving impulses. They remain restless, impulsive, demanding, and unsatisfied. They cling to infantile sources of gratification instead of reaching out for the responsibilities of maturity (p. 264).

Bowlby (1958) investigated the effects of mother child separation. He concluded that some young children, deprived of continuous attention and care from a mother or mother substitute, might suffer persistent, long-term effects, possibly resulting in an inability to form relationships. He submits prolonged separation causes a variety of personality disturbances — the "affectionless character" being the most serious characteristic.

Reeves (1971) considered how adopted and foster children established healthy object relations. He proposed that not securing the biological mother child tie at or near birth hinders the process of primary identification with the mother. He suggests:

> . . . A more tentative proposition, namely that among the pathogenic factors the actual absence of this particular mother for this particular infant can have a detrimental effect on the earliest interactions between them when they come together, with cumulative consequences for the subsequent outcome of the relationship (p. 55).

Goldfarb (1945) compared children in foster care the first three years of their lives, with a similar group institutionalized a comparable time. Many institutionalized children showed a restricted capacity for forming relationships, with aggressive, distractible, and uncontrolled behavior, and impoverished, undifferentiated and passive personalities. A follow up study, though, compared tubercular children, some separated from families by age four, and hospitalized for long periods of time, with a comparison group selected and matched for age and sex. Goldfarb found the differences not as great as had been anticipated. He concludes:

> . . . Some of the workers who first drew attention to the dangers of maternal deprivation resulting from separation have tended on occasion to overstate their case. In particular, statements implying that children who

experience institutionalization and similar forms of severe privation and deprivation in early life commonly develop psychopathic or affectionless characters are incorrect. The results of the present study, however, give no ground for complacency (pp. 247-255).

McWhinnie (1967) studied the age at time of placement of 58 adopted adults and found their age not significantly related to their adjustment, though among those classified as well adjusted, the larger proportion was placed before sixteen weeks. Some case histories did show greater evidence of insecurity when placed after age two.

Witmer, Herzog, Weinstein and Sullivan (1963) found the child's age at placement only slightly associated with later adjustment. Though in a group of 20 — all over 18 months when placed — 45 % made a poor or somewhat poor adjustment compared with 25 to 37 % in other age groups.

Emphasizing the importance of continuity in the earliest and most significant object relationship — that of mother to child — Goldstein, Freud, and Solnit (1973) propose an application of the best interest of the child principle as remedy for alleged adverse consequences inherent in adoption. A procedure that will move the adoptive family in even greater alignment with the procreative family ideal. They suggest that adoption should take place as early as possible, even before the child's birth, and with no trial periods. They avow that " . . . a succession of temporary placements means interruption of early attachments that is so destructive for the child . . . .The adoption decree should be made final and unconditional from the moment a child is placed with a family . . ." (Kramer, 1973, p. 3).

Verrier (1993) asserts an " . . . intuitive understanding . . . " about the relationship between trauma, adopted children, and in-utero bonding (p. xv). "When the natural evolution is interrupted by a postnatal separation from the biological mother, the resultant experience of abandonment and loss is indelibly imprinted upon the unconscious minds of these children, causing that which I call the 'primal wound' " (p. 2). She says, "such inferences can neither be proved nor disproved, only believed or disbelieved" (p. 2). Kirk (1995) calls Verrier's hypothesis [the primal wound] an assault on adoptive family kinship, based on   ". . . a convoluted theory of in womb bonding . . . . by the most dubious evidence . . . that the trauma of separation from the birthmother is irreparable" (p. 20).

Finally, Singer, Brodzinsky, Ramsay, Steir, and Waters (1985) compared the quality of attachment relationships between adoptive and non-adoptive mother infant pairs. They conclude:

> Like non-adoptive mother-infant pairs, most adoptive mothers and their infants develop warm and secure attachment relationships. The initial post delivery bonding, as described by Klaus and Kennell (1976) and others, which is obviously not part of the adoption experience, does not appear to be necessary for the formation of a healthy family relationship. What does seem to be more important is the emergence of caretaking confidence and competence on the part of the parents, and a general caretaking atmosphere that is warm, consistent, and contingent on the needs of the infant. To the extent that adoptive parents develop these characteristics and provide this type of environment, there is little reason to believe their attachment relationships with their young infants will differ markedly from non-adoptive parents (p. 1550).

Resolution of the Oedipal Complex

There are critical periods in the development of any child that may provoke anxiety for a parent or set of parents, whether adoptive or biological. According to analytic theory, the resolution of the oedipal complex is one such situation. The Oedipal complex refers to:

> . . . A characteristic grouping of instinctual drives, aims, object relations and fears universally found at the height of the phallic phase (ages three to six years). During this period the child strives in a limited way for sexual union with the parent of the opposite sex and death or disappearance of the parent of the same sex (Moore & Fine, 1968, p. 66).

Having two sets of parents, says Anderson (1993), suggests adopted children would be theoretically more " . . . prone to split parents into bad adoptive - good biological or vice versa," or, " . . . unable to negotiate oedipal conflicts because of a weakened incest taboo" (p. 145). Tec and Sants (1967) believe that resolution of the oedipal complex is a problem present to all children, but consider it especially difficult and even intensified in adopted children. Resolution of oedipal issues is considered significant to normal as well as pathological development because:

> . . . Genetically, it is a nodal point crucial to the further growth and development of the immediate psychic apparatus . . . In later life . . . dependent on the extent of resolution, it is more or less evident in behavior, attitudes and object choices, and has an important bearing on character structure, the nature of object relationships and sexual identity, fantasy formation and later sexual patterns and activities (Moore & Fine, 1968, p. 66).

Schechter (1960) points out that at the time when the oedipal conflict is at its peak "telling" the young child that he or she is adopted may promote poor identification integration, and foster anxiety about returning to the biological parents, or being abandoned by the adoptive parents. Such anxiety may prolong or prevent resolution of the oedipal conflict in the adopted child. Peller (1961) believes that telling the child around the oedipal age is incompatible with psychoanalytic knowledge. She says:

> . . . Insistent references to his adoption interferes with the full flowering of the oedipal fantasy. This fantasy, with its strong positive and negative affects cannot take its normal course when the child is repeatedly told that he grew inside another lady. The oedipal attachment is predicated on feeling uniquely close to the parent and to consider him tops in everything, in power, wisdom, and love. The oedipal child's thinking is largely governed by primary process thinking, by wishes and fears, inconsistent with one another and incompatible with reality. The introduction of another lady or another set of parents confuses him . . . (p. 149).

But a delay in telling until parents find a more suitable time may be an unrealizable goal. It enhances the possibility that someone else — a classmate, a neighbor, a relative, or a friend reveals the secret, and tells the child first.

Material in support of the view that telling should be delayed until the child is beyond the oedipal stage is very limited, and restricted to isolated clinical examples (Kadushin, 1974). Moreover, Witmer, et al. (1963) contraindicate Schechter and Peller's position. They found a delay in telling was associated with heightened negative reactions by the children themselves. And Brinich (1990) opines " . . . knowledge of adoption

44

[telling] given by loving parents in ways that are 'in step' with their child's emotional and cognitive development is not pathogenic per se" (p. 43).

In reference to the oedipal complex, Easson (1973) proposed that the adopted child has difficulty in three areas of emotional growth: the process of emancipation from his or her adoptive parents; the resolution of incestuous strivings; and identification with the parent of the same sex, and the establishment of a healthy relationship with the parent of the opposite sex.

Schechter (1960) noted that the percentage of adopted children in his practice equaled 13.3 percent as compared with the national average of 0.134 percent (statistics compiled from 29 states). Questions about their birth and beginnings occurred between ages three to six. He said it is a time when " . . . children fantasize a great deal, and, when frustrated by the parents, imagine better parents who could love them and cherish them more . . . " (p. 45).

Theoretically, the oedipal period represents a potential problem area for all children. For the adopted child knowledge that he or she has two sets of parents may complicate resolution of the oedipal complex. Yet, Krugman (1967) suggests " . . . the differentiation to be made is not between two sets of parents ('natural' and 'adoptive') but between parents and those who give birth to the child" (p. 357).

Prolongation of the Family Romance Fantasy

Analysts postulate that adopted children are prone to prolongation of family romance fantasies because they have two sets of parents. Moreover, one set is revealed and the other is hidden. Yet, in the psychiatric literature assumptions about adopted children and family romance fantasies present conflicting reports.

The family romance fantasy is a Freudian construct applicable to a brief, normal state of child development. It is used generically to represent a variety of fantasies including being an adoptive, foster, or stepchild; being separated from, or abandoned by one's birth parents; and fancying having a set of good and ennobled parents, as separate from one's real parents. According to analytic theory, a child fantasizes about being:

> . . . The offspring of other parents who are generally of nobler lineage than his real ones. These new, exalted, and noble parents possess in the fantasy the identical idealized characteristics with which the child had endowed his own parents, during his infantile period. The fantasy comes about because of the discrepancy between his idealized image and the real picture of his parents stemming from the child's observations of defects in them. Thus disillusionment stimulates fantasy that helps to make acceptable the separation and estrangement from parents which is a necessary step in psychic development. Another function of the family romance fantasy is to lessen oedipal guilt by denying the incestuous quality of libidinal feelings toward the parents (Moore & Fine, p. 45).

Clothier (1942) says the family romance fantasy may explain " . . . the apparent complete lack of harmony between the adopted child's personality and his home" (p. 270). She suggests it is a potential pitfall for adopted children because having two sets of parents would make them less able to resolve family romance fantasies. But Lawton and Gross (1964) ask:

> . . . If the child is placed in infancy is not the child exalting the adoptive parents as Freud mentions rather than his natural parents of whom he has had virtually no experience: Are we not attributing cognitive skills to the child that are akin to extrasensory perception? (p. 637)

Kadushin (1974) suggests that all children facing parental rejection fantasize being step or adoptive children, and believe that their real parents are all loving and all accepting. They give up the fantasy when they realize they can both love and hate the parents they have. Moreover, adoptive children can:

> . . . separate the components of this ambivalence by letting one set of parents embody the negative, rejecting component and the other set of parents represent all that is loving and accepting. The task of fusing the two aspects of the parental image is consequently more difficult for the adopted child and the tendency to idealize the unknown biological parent is greater. Yet, the very fact that the first set of parents gave him up for adoption raises doubts in the child's mind about his acceptability, posing a difficulty for the development of a positive self-image (p. 545).

Acceptance of the establishment of the family romance fantasy as a common trait of childhood has been based largely on the conclusions reached by psychoanalysts. Conklin (1920) designed a study to test the validity of the family romance hypothesis. Nine hundred and four students ages fourteen to twenty-five years responded. Twenty-eight percent immediately recall having experienced the fantasy; some recalled experiencing it merely as a daydream. Fifty-four percent of the respondents reported the fantasy had not taken actual form. Fifteen percent believed themselves to be foster children. Eighteen percent had developed ideas of greatness. Greater than half located the fantasy between their eighth and twelfth year. The fantasy endured more than a year for those believing themselves foster children. Twenty-four percent experienced the fantasy less than a year. They most often cited growth, intellectual development, parental familiarity, and physical and mental similarities as cause to extinguish the fantasy (Schwartz, 1970).

Glatzer (1955) suggests the family romance occurs most often between ages eight to twelve, and, " . . . seems to be reinforced in adopted cases" (Sorosky, Baran, & Pannor, 1975, p. 21). Eiduson and Livermore report " . . . the fantasy of family romance . . . is activated when the child is rejected by his adoptive mother" (Lawton & Gross, 1964, p. 637). Kohlsaat and Johnson (1954) opine prolongation of the family romance in adopted children is a function of adoptive parents that " . . . neurotically drive them (adopted children) to such a pitch" (p. 94).

Schwartz (1970) thought the family romance construct lacked empirical support, and designed a study to test if the theory applied to children adopted in infancy. He drew a sample from a larger study comparing an adoptive with a non-adopted peer group. None was from psychiatric or clinical populations. The experimental group consisted of 25 boys placed in adoptive homes before the age of six months. The mean age at placement was three months, with 76 % adopted at three months or earlier. Schwartz compared Thematic Apperception Test responses from the adopted group with the non-adopted control group and found:

> . . . more similarities than differences between the two groups . . . . For the child adopted in infancy, his first allegiance is to the adoptive parents and, within a relatively stable family situation, the family romance is of no greater significance for him than it is for any child (p. 390).

He concludes that there is " . . . no indication that prolongation or fixation of the family romance is a universal characteristic of adopted children" (p. 390). Yet, it is not " . . . that the fantasy can't have some impact in the lives of other adoptees, for example, children adopted at a relatively older age or children brought up in one or more foster homes" (p. 391).

Genealogical Bewilderment

The term genealogical bewilderment is used in the literature on adopted children and identity formation to describe a hypothetical state of distress and confusion they experience by having no information, limited information, or conflicted information about their family of origin. How the adopted child — that is missing his or her genealogical information — is able to resolve the primary developmental tasks of late adolescence and early adulthood, theoretically a period of psychosocial development concerned with identity formation, remains of substantial interest.

The word identity derives from the Latin "idem" meaning the same, as in the " . . . sameness of essential character; sameness in all that constitutes the objective reality of a thing; selfsameness; oneness" (Abend, 1974, p. 607). Erikson (1968) says man's search for identity is a search for continuity and sameness. The problem is that identity must establish a continuity between society's past and future, and adolescence, with all its vulnerability and power, is the critical transformer of both. The American Psychoanalytic Association defines identity as:

> The experience of the self as a unique coherent entity which is continuous and remains the same despite inner psychic and outside environmental changes. The sense of identity begins with the child's awareness that he exists as an individual in a world with outer objects . . . eventually . . . an integrated self-representation (self-image) is created out of the multiple former identifications contributing to character traits (Moore & Fine, 1968, p. 50).

But, Hoopes (1990) suggests that prior to an exploration of identity formation in adopted children " . . . look at the social phenomenon of adoption, since an understanding of the complexity of the adoption process may help in interpretation of the clinical and research literature" (p. 147).

The foundation of the concept of sameness rests upon consanguinity. For the adopted child there is none. Adoption policy and practice severs the child's ancestral connections. In place of his or her heritage, he or she receives substitute bloodlines intended to be socially equivalent. An American Academy of Pediatrics, Committee on Adoptions (1971) report suggests the adopted child's need for knowledge of ancestry is too often unrecognized, or suppressed by both the child and his parents.

> There is ample evidence that the adopted child retains the need for seeking his ancestry for a long time. What he is really seeking is to achieve a unity and persistence of personality in spite of the break in the continuity of his life. The struggle with this problem may reach its peak in adolescence and, in the extreme, result in running away in search of real parents (p. 949).

The report acknowledges the adopted child's need for ancestral information, yet appears influenced by the clinical observations of Schechter and Tousseing, as found in the psychoanalytic literature on adopted children. Schechter (1960) notes that some adolescent adoptees start "roaming" — aimlessly seeking the fantasized good and real parents — while having difficulties rebelling against their adoptive parents. Similarly, Tousseing writes in a letter to Schechter that:

> The adolescence of adopted children seems to be a particularly difficult one because it is harder for adoptive adolescents to accept their rebellion against the adoptive parents, to give them up as love objects. Furthermore, I have now seen a number of cases in which children in adolescence start roaming almost aimlessly, though sometimes they are aware that they are seeking someone or something (Schechter, 1960, p. 30).

Frisk (1964) found that ego development, identification, and identity formation in adopted children was prone to complications. His observations come from a study of 19 foster children attending the Outpatient Clinic for Teenagers in Helsingfors. All were between 14 and 17 years of age, and adopted during their first year of life. He said:

> It became important for these children to learn about their biological parents, what they looked like, while searching for common features between the parents and themselves. The question of the purpose of their birth became a burning problem arising when they realized they were not like their foster-parents. They experienced an emptiness within themselves; they lacked essential facts for the building up of their ego and identity (p. 8).

Relating the experience to Erikson's psychosocial theory, Frisk notes that these children could not find themselves because by not knowing the facts of their genetic origins they lacked a true genetic concept. He concludes:

> When the "genetic identity" is obscured one does not know what is passed on. These unknown factors breed feelings of insecurity and inferiority. Even if identity confusion is a fact in practically all adolescents towards the conclusion of adolescence, it appears that self-identification in the adopted child is far more complicated than in children who live under normal conditions. Apart from other essential environmental factors, emphasis must be laid on the obscure "genetic ego" (p. 11).

Kornitzer (1971) suggests adolescent adoptee identity formation is impaired because knowledge of an essential part is cut off, and remains on the other side of the adoption barrier (Sorosky, et. al, 1975). Sants (1964) says:

> In adoption of children there is in most cases an implicit attempt to transplant the child from his natural family into his substitute family . . . such a graft can never be completely carried out; roots in the natural family can never be severed without trace (p. 133).

In effect, adoption deprives the child of a genetic ego so there is no help when he or she strives to resolve problems of identity. The many unknown facts create conflict, confusion, and distorted fantasies (Sants, 1964). In this sense the:

> . . . genealogically bewildered child . . . either has no knowledge of natural parents or only uncertain knowledge of them. The resulting state of confusion and uncertainty . . . fundamentally undermines . . . security and thus affects [the adoptee's] . . . mental health (Sants, 1964, p. 140).

Sants associates adopted adolescence, the development of poor self-esteem, and a confused sense of identity with a state of genealogic bewilderment. Wellisch (1952) suggests:

> . . . knowledge of and definite relationship to his genealogy is therefore necessary for a child to build up his complete body image and world picture. It is an inalienable and entailed right of every person. There is an urge, a call in everybody to follow the tradition of his family, race, nation, and the religious community into which he is born. The loss of this tradition is a deprivation that may result in the stunting of emotional development . . . . It is understandable that there are cases of maladjustment in children which show that the deprivation of a child's knowledge of his genealogy can have harmful consequences (p. 42).

Yet, Hoopes (1990) concludes identity formation and adoption are:

> . . . complex experiences with multiple interlocking family and social inputs. Research has identified some of the variables that influence identity formation . . . . many of the same variables are important to the biological child . . . . It is totally possible for the adopted adolescent to achieve a mature identity if the factors outlined above [family relationship, communication about adoption, and parental attitudes about adoption] are present in the family . . . (pp. 165-166).

Finally, Goebel and Lott (1986) suggest adoptees may have to work harder at the task of achieving identity — hence perhaps they master it even better than non-adoptees.

The Meaning of Search

Perhaps nowhere does the psychiatric literature on the adopted child represent a greater confluence of imagination, interpretation, and psychoanalytic theory, politics, social attitudes, child welfare principles, and adoption practice than over the meaning of search. Presumptions about the searcher's motivations — their unhappiness (Aumend & Barrett, 1984), dissatisfaction, low self-concept, and low self-esteem (Aumend & Barrett, 1984; Sobol & Cardiff, 1983) — become the parameters that define them. The selection of these research parameters suggests an underlying hypothesis of abnormality and deviance. Schechter and Bertocci (1990) affirm:

> Adoption personnel have a priori tended to question the normality and stability of the adoptee-searcher (Haines & Timms, 1985). . . . Pervasive irrational anxieties about relinquishment exist in the social unconsciousness and are manifest in the prevailing atmosphere of distrust . . . (Small, 1979). Attending hostilities . . . become projected onto the adoptee . . . prejudging [them] as potentially intrusive, retributive and so on (p. 87).

Further, there are persistent and presumptive attitudes that " . . . the need to search implies . . . criticism of the adoptive family, or a wish to have remained with the birthparent" (Schechter & Bertocci, 1990, pp. 87-88). But, the:

> . . . clashing of views . . . tends to obfuscate a more dispassionate and probing attempt to understand, from . . . the adopted person, what the need to search really means . . . . For . . . adoptees confronting this phenomenon, . . . thwarting . . . their attempts to establish a full personal

history creates a particular anguish virtually unknown in
any other psychosocial context" (Schechter & Bertocci,
1990, p. 62).

Adoptees in search of their origins are a relatively recent phenomenon, whereas interest in ancestry, heredity, and genealogy is not. It originates in antiquity. The sealing of birth and adoption records began in the late 1930's. The first generation of adopted children affected by clean break legislation reached their majority in the 1960's. When they began their quest, they discovered that access to information concerning their heritage was blocked.

Florence Fisher's 1973 book, *The Search for Anna Fisher*, details the societally instigated obstacles, and degree of difficulty that she and other adoptees in search encounter. The Adoptee Liberty Movement Association (ALMA) that she founded spearheaded efforts by adopted adults to repeal clean break legislation.

Earliest efforts to explain the meaning of search come mostly from clinical reports based on psychoanalytically oriented treatment of adopted children and adolescents. Not surprisingly, these reports connect adoptive status, the meaning of search, and adopted children to psychopathology, not genealogy.

Assumptions about the searchers inner world, and whether search is symbolic or activated, or relates to loss, mourning, jealousy or envy, or is about complications in sexual or identity development, search ideation, cognitive dissonance, or internalization of the locus of control, appear to be exercises in fitting subject to theory.

Data regarding numbers, gender, and ages of searchers remains speculative. Triseliotis and Hill (1990) suggest recent " . . . publicity focused on . . . 'origins' and 'roots' . . . and the emphasis on minority rights . . . helped to generate . . . greater consciousness among all people . . . about genealogy" (p. 117). Now more adoptees are " . . . likely to be searching for their origins out of curiosity. . . Public opinion and, in some countries, the law . . . sanction search for information or contact without generating a sense of guilt, betrayal, or shame" (p. 117).

Kadushin and Martin's (1988) definition further confuses the meaning of search. "Search is defined as the efforts of either adult adoptee or the birth parent to secure identifying information that might possibly lead to locating the other party" (p. 580). This perspective places the emphasis on a "reunion" between the birthparent and child. Framing search that way means that each has an equal need for information for finding one another. Kadushin and Martin's interpretation does not grant the adopted persons need to know their heritage as primary. Finally, they say:

> As a result of a better understanding of the motives of adoptees seeking information about, or reunification with, their birth parents and of the outcome of these reunions, it is generally agreed that freer access to non identifying background information should be granted and that this approach should be augmented by updated information that can be made available either to the biological parent or the adopted child (p. 587).

A number of studies focus on the differences between adoptee searchers and non-searchers. It would be interesting to determine whether similar differences would be found among non-adopted persons that do genealogical searches and those that do not. Would research parameters include the extent of the searcher's curiosity; level of family conflict; satisfaction with their family of origin; identity development; self-concept; and level of happiness?

Outcomes

Adoption is a social construct, its policies and practices consonant with the culture's prevailing political, economic, religious, and moral values. Society devalues adoption. It adjudges adoption to be "second best," or, "second choice," because it fails to measure up to procreation. Moreover, the association of adoption with bastardy is endemic. It perseveres and prevails. People learn early on that the adopted child is "different." He or she comes from "bad seed," and is "damaged goods." The omnipresent perception that adoptive family structure is deficient, and thereby lacking, wanting, or functionally impaired, and that the adopted child is faulty, flawed, and in need of reformation or treatment associates adoption with mal-adaptation. People know little about adoption, but they do know this.

Clinical observations of adopted children brought to analytically oriented therapists by their adoptive parents form the basis for many of the quotations in this paper. This does not justify the conclusion that adopted children were or are more disturbed or maladapted than non-adopted children. Only that adoptive parents, for whatever reason, appear to bring their adoptive children to clinicians more often than do non-adoptive parents.

Empirical research is limited in quantity, quality, and scope. It has been difficult, even impossible, to verify the theoretical formulations empirically.

Nevertheless, biased, stigmatic, and stereotypic thinking, beliefs, opinions, attitudes, and myths about the adopted child proliferate, and endure. Oddly, to be born out of wedlock is not the same as being adopted. The culture only profiles the child once the fact of his or her adoption is made known. We remain short on empirical references and cross validation, and long on theory, opinion, and speculation.

References

Abend, S. M. (1974). Problems of identity: Theoretical and clinical applications. *Psychoanalytic Quarterly, 43*, 606-637.

American Academy of Pediatrics. (1971). Identity development in adopted children. *Pediatrics, 47*, 948-949.

Anderson, R. (1993). *Second choice.* Chesterfield, MO: Badger Hill Press.

Aumend, S., & Barrett, M. (1984). Self-concept and attitudes toward adoption: A comparison of searching and non-searching adult adoptees. *Child Welfare, 63*, 251-259.

Bohman, M., & Sigvardsson, S. (1990). Outcomes in adoption: lessons from longitudinal studies. In D. M. Brodzinsky & M. D. Schechter (Eds.), *The psychology of adoption* (pp. 93-106). New York: Oxford University Press.

Bowlby, J. (1958). The nature of the child's tie to his mother. *International Journal of Psychoanalysis, 39*, 211-247.

Brinich, P. M. (1990). Adoption from the inside out: a psychoanalytic perspective. In D. M. Brodzinsky & M. D. Schechter (Eds.), *The psychology of adoption* (pp. 42-61). New York: Oxford University Press.

Brodzinsky, D. M. (1990). A stress and coping model of adoption adjustment. In D. M. Brodzinsky & M. D. Schechter (Eds.), *The psychology of adoption* (pp. 3-24). New York: Oxford University Press.

Brodzinsky, D. M., & Schechter, M. D. (1990). Preface. In D. M. Brodzinsky & M. D. Schechter (Eds.), *The psychology of adoption* (pp. ix-xiii). New York: Oxford University Press.

Cadoret, R. J. (1990). Biologic perspectives of adoptee adjustment. In D. M. Brodzinsky & M. D. Schechter (Eds.), *The psychology of adoption* (pp 25-41). New York: Oxford University Press.

Carey, W. B. (1974). Adopting children: the medical aspects. *Children Today, 3,* 10-15.

Clothier, F. (1942). Placing the child for adoption. *Mental Hygiene, 26,* 257-274.

Clothier, F. (1943). The psychology of the adopted child. *Mental Hygiene, 27,* 222-230.

Conklin, E. S. (1920). The foster-child fantasy. *American Journal of Psychology, 31,* 59-76.

Downs, S. W., Moore, E., McFadden, E. J., & Costin, L. B (2000*). Child welfare and family services* (6th. ed.). Boston: Allyn & Bacon.

Easson, W. (1973, July). Special sexual problems of the adopted adolescent. *Medical Aspects of Human Sexuality,* 92-105.

Eiduson, B. T., & Livermore, J. B. (1953). Complications in therapy with adopted children. *American Journal of Orthopsychiatry, 23,* 795-802.

Erikson, E. H. (1968). *Identity: Youth and crisis.* New York: Norton.

Feder, L. (1974). Adoption trauma: Oedipus myth/clinical reality. *International Journal of Psychoanalysis, 55,* 143-171.

Fisher, F. (1973). *The search for Anna Fisher.* New York: Arthur Fields.

Frisk, M. (1964). Identity problems and confused conceptions of the genetic ego in adopted children during adolescence. *Acta Paedo Psychiatric*a, *31,* 6-12.

Glatzer, H. T. (1955). Adoption and delinquency. *Nervous Child, 11,* 52-56.

Goldfarb, W. (1945). Psychological privation in infancy and psychological adjustment. *American Journal of Orthopsychiatry, 15,* 247-255.

Goldstein, J., Freud, A., & Solnit, A. (1973). *Beyond the best interests of the child.* London: Free Press.

Hartman, A., & Laird, J. (1990). Family treatment after adoption. In D. M. Brodzinsky & M. D. Schechter (Eds.), *The psychology of adoption* (pp. 221-239). New York: Oxford University Press.

Hoopes, J. L. (1990). Adoption and identity formation. In D. M. Brodzinsky & M. D. Schechter (Eds.), *The psychology of adoption* (pp. 144-166). New York: Oxford University Press.

Jaffee, B., & Fanshall, D. (1970). *How they fared in adoption: A follow-up study.* New York: Columbia University Press.

Kadushin, A. (1974). *Child welfare services.* (2nd. ed.). New York: Macmillan.

Kadushin, A., & Martin, J. A. (1988). *Child welfare services.* (4th. ed.). New York: Macmillan

Kirk, H. D. (1964). *Shared fate.* New York: The Free Press.

Kirk, H. D. (1995). *Looking back, looking forward: An adoptive father's sociological testament.* Indianapolis: Perspectives Press.

Kirschner, D., & Nagel, L. S. (1998). Antisocial behavior in adoptees: Patterns and dynamics. *Child and Adolescent Social Work, 5, 4,* 300-314.

Kohlsaat, B., & Johnson, A. (1954). Some suggestions for practice in infant adoption. *Social Casework, 35,* 91-99.

Kornitzer, M. (1971). The adopted adolescent and the sense of identity. *Child Adoption, 66,* 43-48.

Kramer, R. (1973, October).The psychological parent is the real parent. *The New York Times Magazine.*

Krugman, D. C. (1967). Differences in the relation of parents and children to adoption. *Child Welfare, 46,* 267-71.

Lawton, J,. & Gross, S. (1964). Review of psychiatric literature on adopted children. *Archives of General Psychiatry, 11,* 633-644.

References

McWhinnie, A. M. (1967). *Adopted children and how they grew up.* London: Routledge & Kegan Paul.

Moore, B., & Fine, B. (1968). *A glossary of psychoanalytic terms and concepts.* New York: The American Psychoanalytic Association.

Paton, J. M. (1954). *The adopted break silence.* Action, CA: Life History Study Center.

Peller, L. (1961). About "telling the child" about his adoption. *Bulletin of the Philadelphia Association for Psychoanalysts, 11,* 145-154.

Raymond, L., & Dywasuk, C. (1974). *Adoption and after.* New York: Harper & Row, Publishers.

Reeves, A. C. (1971). Children with surrogate parents: cases seen in analytic therapy and an aetiological hypothesis. *British Journal of Medical Psychology, 44,* 155-171.

Sants, H. J. (1964). Genealogical bewilderment in children with substitute parents. *British Journal of Medical Psychology, 37,* 133-141.

Schechter, M. D. (1960). Observations on adopted children. *Archives of General Psychiatry, 3,* 21-32.

Schechter, M. D., & Bertocci, D (1990). The meaning of search. In D. M. Brodzinsky & M. D. Schechter (Eds.), *The psychology of adoption* (pp. 62-90). New York: Oxford University Press.

Schwartz, E. (1970, July). The family romance fantasy in children adopted in infancy. *Child Welfare, 49,* 386-391.

Singer, L. M., Brodzinsky, D. M., Ramsay, D., Steir, M., & Waters, E. (1985). Mother-infant attachment in adoptive families. *Child Development, 56,* 1543-1551.

Small, J. W. (1977). *A comparison of genetic identity indicators between adopted and non-adopted adults.* Unpublished masters thesis, The Catholic University of America, Washington, DC.

Small, J. W. (1987). Working with adoptive families. *Public Welfare, 45,* 33-41.

Sobol, M., & Cardiff, J. (1983). A sociopsychological investigation of adult adoptees search for birth parents. *Family Relations, 32,* 447-483.

Sorosky, A. D., Baran A., & Pannor, R. (1975). Identity conflicts in adoptees. *American Journal of Orthopsychiatry, 45,* 18-27.

Tec, L., & Gordon, S. (1967). The adopted child's adaptation to adolescence. *American Journal of Orthopsychiatry, 37,* 402.

Toussieng, P. W. (1962). Thoughts regarding the etiology of psychological difficulties in adopted children. *Child Welfare, 41,* 59-65.

Triseliotis, J., & Hill, M. (1990). Contrasting adoption and foster care, and residential rearing. In D. M. Brodzinsky & M. D. Schechter (Eds.), *The psychology of adoption* (pp. 107-120). New York: Oxford University Press.

Verrier, N. N. (1993). *The primal wound.* Understanding the adopted child. Baltimore: Gateway Press.

Wade, J. W. (1968). Adoption. In W. H. Nault (Ed. et al), *The world book encyclopedia* (p.56). Chicago: Field Enterprises Educational Corporation.

Weinstein, E. (1968). Adoption. In D. L. Sills (Ed.), *International encyclopedia of the social sciences* (1st ed.). London: Macmillan/The Free Press.

Wellisch, E. (1952). Children without genealogy: A problem of adoption. *Mental Health, 13,* 41-42.

Witmer, H. L., Herzog, E., Weinstein, E. A., & Sullivan, M. E. (1963). *Independent adoptions.* New York: Russell Sage Foundation.

Working with Adoptive Families

Children that are biologically unrelated to their parents come into families differently than do children born to their parents. They come into families through a social and legal process, rather than by birth. Through the process of adoption, children become children of adoption and parents become adoptive parents. Often the feelings, attitudes, and behaviors of adoptive family members are inconsistent with the expectations underlying traditional adoption practice. The relationship between these inconsistencies, children adopted and raised by parents that are biologically unrelated to them, and adoptive family dysfunction is the subject of this paper.

Historically, there has been a tendency to treat adoption as though it were a disease. "Out of wedlock pregnancy was seen as a symptom of some psychological need—conflict with a dominant mother, lack of response from a passive father, a desire for self-punishment," or, " . . . an attempt at self assertion and independence" (Kadushin, 1974, p. 484). Psychoanalyst Povl Toussieng (1962) suggests adoptive parent's unresolved resistance to parenthood causes emotional conflicts in their adoptive children. Disturbances in early object relations, prolongation of family romance fantasies, and genealogical bewilderment are considered symptoms of pathology indigenous to adopted children. Consequently, the child has become the unit of treatment.

This view, as well as our choice of terms reflects a social bias. People say adopted child in much the same way as they identify an epileptic or diabetic child. By placing the word adopted before the word child, our associations are with the conditions that precede an adoption, like abandonment, rejection, and illegitimacy. But we apply different standards for social conditions like alcoholism or divorce. There we say children of alcoholics or children of divorce. Terms like child, children, or adult children of adoption more appropriately indicate that adoption, like marriage and divorce, is a socially created condition, and not a disease.

Until the 1970's white, infertile couples could turn to adoption as a solution to childlessness. Correspondingly, white, unmarried mothers surrendered their infants to adoption. There was a match between the supply of infants and the desire to adopt. Much has changed in the past 30 years. Negative attitudes toward mothers that keep their babies have softened. The pill makes it possible for women to have sex without pregnancy. Abortion is a woman's constitutional right. Individuals now consider adopting older children, as well as interracial infants, and may choose an inter-country, private, or open adoption.

Before the 1940's, U. S. child adoptions were less secret and more open. Birth and adoption records generally were not sealed. Many state adoption laws were modeled on an 1851 Massachusetts statute intended to " . . . provide evidence of the legal transfer of a child by the biological parents to the adopting parents and provision for a public record of the transfer" (The Child and The State, 1938, p. 165). But the spirit of openness that characterized earlier child adoptions moved toward secrecy. Concepts like nurture versus nature and the melting pot theory led to a belief that in the adoption of a child environment could supersede nature. Adoptive family influence became more important than that of the child's hereditary family. Belief in the supremacy of nurture over nature formed the basis for the fantasy that the child's ancestry could be denied. It became necessary to find ways to foster and protect the fantasy. Hence, adoption policy moved toward secrecy and practice moved toward protection. A 1951 State of Mississippi Adoption Survey advocated a " . . . clean break between the relationship of the natural parents and the child in order that the child may become completely a part of his [her] new family" (p. 20). The practice of sealing birth and adoption records was an attempt to effect a break between the child and his or her hereditary history and genetic origins. Sealing a record removes it from public inspection. Once sealed, only judicial sanction and good cause can open birth or adoption records. The practice of sealing birth and adoption records has largely gone unchanged since the late 1930's.

Children of adoption are subjects of intense interest, ample speculation, and much ignorance. Knowledge is largely unavailable because traditions of secrecy, protection, or denial make it difficult to obtain data. Much less attention is given the child's developmental environment, the adoptive parent-child bond, adoptive family minority status, and society's condemnation of adoption (Schwan & Tuskam, 1979, p. 345). The adopted child has been isolated as though he or she were a specimen out of context. Flawed thinking based on an unsound belief system makes us forget that a child is a child first, and adoption happens second. Faulty thinking reckons that an adopted child did not exist before adoption, and unlike all other children he or she is neither conceived, nor born, and has no ancestry and no past. This is the fundamental adoption myth. Some children of adoption and their parents believe it. Adoption practice has institutionalized it. Let us look at how belief in the myth may affect adoptive family dysfunction.

Denying the Differences

All children of adoption have two sets of parents—birth parents and adoptive parents. Blood ties and a common ancestry connect them to their birth parents in a way that is not possible with their adoptive parents. This difference in adoptive family structure is accepted, minimized, or denied by adoptive parents and children. "Denial refers to the automatic and involuntary exclusion from awareness of some disturbing aspect of reality or the inability to acknowledge its true significance" (White & Gilliland, 1973, p. 78).

Some adoptive parents desire to see themselves the same as non-adoptive parents. Yet, when that desire leads a parent to deny that there are any differences, that may indicate an unwholesome defense against the realities of adoptive parenting. Seeing themselves the same as non-adoptive parents promotes unrealistic expectations for themselves and their children. Children of adoption may similarly long to be the same as non-adopted children, and to share a common ancestry and blood ties with their adoptive parents. What is it about being different that leads adoptive family members to deny these differences?

Traditional adoptive families are structured out of loss. Infertile couples lose the fulfillment, status and self-esteem that often accompany reproductive parenthood, and the symbolic procreative child their adoptive son or daughter can never be. Friends and relatives suggest that the couple go on a holiday, tell them to "try a little harder," or ask them, "Why not adopt"? The emotional impact of infertility may be devastating, and may have a negative effect on the adoptive family system. Family therapist Virginia Satir (1972) believes that low self-esteem in the marital subsystem is a basis for family dysfunction. Adoptive couples may receive little or no help with the emotional effects of infertility, as they often lack peer and familial support and understanding. Parents that chose to adopt through agencies report that when workers asked them if they had resolved the emotional effects of infertility, all knew enough to answer "yes." Adoption is a way for infertile couples to have a family. It is not a cure for infertility. Individuals may find their way to self-help groups like "Resolve," a national infertility, education, and support organization.

Adopted persons lose their connection to their ancestry and their genetic identity. Being disconnected from one's ancestry is akin to the amputation of a limb. It is not there, but it leaves a phantom presence. This cosmic experience leaves its victim feeling an unparalleled loneliness that comes with not belonging the same as others. Adoptive status always means a loss of social status. But the expectation is that children that gain parents through adoption will deny any losses. Loss brings grief, but the significance of adoptive family loss often goes unrecognized.

Denial and Adoptive Families

Potentially much denial surrounds the fact of adoption in adoptive families. Some family members deny that the child was not born to the parents, and develop strategies to defend the fiction. Consequently, the child's basic sense of self develops around a flawed belief system that perceives the experience of being born to one's parents the same as being adopted. These family members may become co-dependents to a denial process that is analogous to co-dependence that occurs in alcoholic families (Co-Dependency, 1984; Seixas & Youcha, 1985; Woititz, 1983).

The tem co-dependence was originally used to describe the effects on the life of someone that is involved with a chemically dependent person, like an alcoholic. Co-dependence is defined more broadly now as a dysfunctional pattern of living and problem solving that is grounded in denial. Co-dependent families engage in patterns of behavior designed to minimize or totally deny a familial reaction to a painful reality (Subby & Friel, 1984, pp. 31-32). Co-dependent family systems nurture a pattern of denial through sets of unwritten and unspoken rules (p. 32). "It is what happens to family members when they try to adapt to a . . . family system that seeks to protect and enable . . . " (Wegscheider-Cruse, 1984, p. 1). Whitfield (1984) suggests that defenses used to some degree by all persons, " . . . become exaggerated due to . . . increased stresses and double binds . . . " (p. 46). Often the feelings, attitudes, and behaviors of adoptive family members are inconsistent with the expectations underlying traditional adoption practice. Co-dependence in adoptive families may be manifest when:

- The family structures itself around a problem. The child's out of wedlock birth and illegitimate status, the effects of the "bad seed myth," or the couple's inability to attain reproductive parenthood are perceived as deficits that the family should try to overcome.

- The family tries to hide the problem. The adoptive family attempts to structure itself as though it were a procreative family.

- Family members have difficulty identifying and expressing feelings about adoption.

70

- There is a tendency toward perfectionism and unrealistic expectations.

- Communications that relate to adoption are faulty. They are often confusing, inconsistent, and emotional, and reflect a denial of reality.

- Fantasy replaces reality.

- Adoption related attitudes and behaviors tend to become rigid.

- Family members experience feelings of powerlessness over their lives, like having lost control over what has happened to them, and not having had an opportunity to make a choice.

- Family members feel responsible for the behavior and feelings of other family members, and try to make up for something that is missing.

- Family members share a basic sense of shame or low self-esteem.

- Family members show a strong need for approval from others both in the family, and the social system.

We may gain an understanding of how these patterns of denial occur by exploring characteristics that are common to all traditional adoptive families. Infertile couples start with a strike against them—disappointment over their failure to reproduce. Andrews (1979) found that the strong societal approval given procreative parenting could cause infertile, adoptive couples to feel an even greater degree of differentness or inferiority. Adoptive parents may feel disappointment that their child will never be a biological extension of themselves. Some adopted children become the outward symbol of their parent's self-esteem. Parents that consider adoption is "second best" may over invest in their child's achievements as a means of compensation. The child may feel worthy only because of superior performance or achievement.

The adoption process places people in a supplicant role. Adopting couples must pass a home study. If they meet the criteria for "perfect parents," they may be vulnerable to an expectation for perfection, thereby denying any adoption-related problems. Child welfare treated adoption as a one-time service provided to the child. The child was bestowed a new identity, and his or her birth record was sealed, disconnecting links between the child's past and future. But child welfare's emphasis on secrecy contributes to the denial of differences between adoptive and procreative parenting. In an attempt to live up to expectations underlying traditional adoption practice parent and child make believe. Examples of unspoken and unwritten family rules (Subby & Friel, 1984, pp. 36-41) designed to protect parents and children from adoptive family realities include:

- Adoption is not a topic for family discussion. An adoptive parent says: "Johnny never asks any questions. I don't even think he thinks about it. As soon as we got him home, we forget about it, too. We already told him that he was adopted when he was young, so he knows."

- Admitting the family has an adoption-related problem is not permissible. That would let others know that an adoptive family is not the same as a non-adoptive family. "As far as I'm concerned, they are my real parents, and I don't care if I ever know anything about her."

- Feelings related to adoptive family status are not permissible because adoption does not feel any different. "Two months after we adopted Johnny I forgot all about his being adopted. It's as if it never happened."

- Communications about adoption should be indirect or oblique. "We have Johnny, our adopted son, and two daughters of our own."

- Substitute fantasies for realities: "Your mother loved you so much she gave you up to be adopted."

- Special conditions apply to adoptive status: "You are looking for your mother? Why would you want to do that"? "Your child is adopted? Oh, how wonderful of you to adopt him"!

- Be careful whom you trust. "If I tell her about her mother I'm afraid she will be promiscuous, too." "We told him his parents were killed in a car accident." "I just didn't ask the social worker any questions. That way, when she asks, I'll just tell her I don't know." "If I tell them I am searching, I believe it will kill them"!

- It is better to censor the facts about adoption than to feel guilt, fear, or shame. "We are Jewish, and we raised him that way. I have never told him that his parents were not Jewish. But he keeps asking me over and over."

- Do not rock the boat. "I have no interest in knowing who my real parents are." "We will tell her, but I don't think she is old enough yet. Maybe when she is ten."

Co-dependent behavior may be a problem among helping professionals. Wegscheider-Cruse describes the "professional enabler" as " . . . any helping professional who engages in the same kinds of dysfunctional behavior as the family—avoidance, protecting, covering up, denial, and taking responsibility for someone else" (Whitfield, 1984, p. 51). School counselors, juvenile justice workers, and health professionals claim they have a higher percentage of children from adoptive homes in their caseloads. Some professionals fail to acknowledge adoptive family differences, or are uncomfortable exploring adoptive family issues. A colleague that worked in a drug abuse center commented on the number of adoptive families they served, but when asked what happened when adoptive family issues came up said, "Oh! We don't touch that."

The Task of Telling

How, when and what to tell a child about their adoption is open to question. There are many opinions on the subject. Experts suggest different ages and developmental stages. Some advocate not telling. The difficulty associated with informing children of their adoptive status tells much about how society perceives adoption. If telling children about their adoption were perceived as "goods news," the difficulty would be obviated. People want to shout good news from the rooftops. But feelings about adoption tend to be ambivalent, and range from joy to shame.

Telling is customarily the parent's responsibility. Consequently, parent's personal attitudes toward adoption are most likely to determine what, how, when and if they choose to tell. Telling may represent painful associations with infertility. Some parents never seem able to find the right words or the right time. Some choose not to tell. For others, it may be like telling children about sex. These parents deliver the message quickly, without discussion, and only once. Often when parents do not tell, someone else does. A physician (Livingston, 1977) found out at age 34 that he was adopted. Everyone else in the family knew. Following a search he said, "In this vast land I sought a person whose face I would not recognize, whose name I did not know: my mother" (p. 85). An editor found out at age 46 that he was adopted. Every one else in his family knew. Although he learned his birthmother had died in childbirth he succeeded in finding other relatives.

He said, " . . . to see people who look and act like you . . . . to know where you are in the family tree. To know my roots gives me full identity" (Haase, 1977, p. 7). A man of 70 discovered he was adopted when he started a genealogical search.

Satir (1972) suggests withholding information and keeping adoption a secret is like other family secrets. Most are based on fear and shame, and often rationalized as "protection of the kids" (p. 107). Not telling—or telling in a hurried and self-conscious way—communicates to the child that adoptive status is so bad it is not a matter for discussion. It is a short jump from that message to an understanding that children of adoption must be bad, too. Children learn what being adopted means through the eyes of others.

They ask their parents to tell them what happened. "Where is she"? "What is her name"? "Where is she now"? "What does she do"? They want to know whom they look like and what "she" looks like. Children that sense their parent's discomfort with questions about their birth families and their adoption will stop making inquiries. Some come to understand that asking questions places them at risk for invoking their parent's anger, disapproval, and rejection. If their adoptive parents believe that talking about adoption is not "good," then adoption must not be good. And being adopted must not be good. Consequently, the child may conclude, "If I am adopted I must not be 'good' either."

Adopted children learn they are different when people speak of adoption through metaphors. For example, some refer to a birthmother as "the woman in whose body you grew" or "that lady" or simply as "she" or "her" instead of mother. They hear people talk about their "real family" or their "real parents" instead of saying birth family or birthparents. People tell adopted children that, "your mother loved you so much she gave you away."

Adoption metaphors deny reality. Substituting terms like that "lady," "her," or "she" for mother tells adopted children that they are unlike all other human children that are born to mothers. So adopted children gain no validation for the truth—that like their peers they too are born to mothers. Similarly, telling children that someone gave them up for adoption because they loved them so much does not validate the child's reality. A child holds on to a cherished toy or blanket with a tenacity that is born of possession.

On a scale rating rejection experiences from one through ten one's mother giving them away would probably rate a ten. Parents attempt to explain the rejection away. "She was too young." "They were college students." Nonetheless, explanations cannot undo the child's reality. Adoption's association with issues like abandonment and rejection makes some people uncomfortable enough that they attempt to deny their significance. But adopted children may need to validate their experience. When validation is not forthcoming, they may begin to mistrust their sense of what to them is real, meaningful, and significant. Some adopted children learn not to share their hurts, worries, and concerns with others. They learn to discount and repress their feelings. Some learn not to feel anything about their adoption. Parents that deny that adoption is different are emotionally unavailable to their children, and exacerbate their children's sense of isolation.

A 3-year-old child runs home in tears. "I don't like 'dopted. I don't want 'dopted," she tells her mother. For many growing up adopted involves feelings that are difficult to identify and hard to express—including a sense of isolation—because their mother gave them away—their parents can't have children of their own—other's disapprove of them—they have no idea who they look like, where and who they come from—who they are, who they will become—they don't belong in ways that all other's belong.

Adult Children of Adoption

Adult children of adoption grow up knowing that their birthmothers gave them up. They are aware that the adoption process disconnected them from their beginnings. They are generally sensitive about the subject of adoption. They often report that they knew few if any other adopted persons and rarely talked about adoption while growing up. They disagree on the importance of search. Often their first significant exposure to the experiences of other adopted persons comes from a search and support group meeting or via membership on an internet newsletter.

Many adopted persons want to know their name, religious background, ethnicity, and health history. They want to see if they look like members of their birth family. Most say they are not searching for mothers and fathers. They say their mothers and fathers are the parents that raised them. They want to find out about themselves—their heredity, genetic identity—their roots. Most are sensitive to their adoptive parent's feelings. Many say they are afraid to ask them for information about their adoption and generally do not tell their parents that they are searching. Many say wanting to search makes them feel guilty—like they are betraying their adoptive parents—

whose feelings they wish to protect—but that they plan to tell their parents after they complete a search.

All adult children of adoption have to cope with negative attitudes toward their adoptive status including those expressed by friends, family, neighbors, and the media. Some are acts of omission, as when the family excludes an adopted grandchild from an outing that includes all non-adopted cousins. Adult children of adoption may be lawyers, doctors, nurses, construction workers, salespersons, editors, teachers, and social workers. Some still say, "I am an adopted child."

Family Roles

Satir (1972) found that troubled families engage in universal patterns of response to avoid the threat of rejection, including: placating (trying to please, never disagreeing, avoiding any response that makes others mad); blaming (finding fault, dictating, holding others responsible); computing (allowing for no semblance of feelings, always remaining cool and calm, and making no mistakes); and distracting (always responding irrelevantly to what others say or do) (pp. 62-70). Wegscheider-Cruse (1984) describes a variety of roles that enable children to function in co-dependent families. These include the family hero, the family scapegoat, and the lost child. They are not all-inclusive, tend to overlap, and are performed to varying degrees of intensity. Similarly, many adopted persons that engage in behaviors that shield themselves and their parents from experiencing the full impact and consequences of adoptive family status may ultimately become beholden to a denial process.

Family heroes usually place the needs of their parents ahead of their own. For example, in *National Adoptalk* Wendy Hollenbach wrote, "No questions haunt me. I know who I am and I know who my parents are. They are Dr. and Mrs. Harry G. Hollenbach" (1973, p. 1). Lifton (1979) refers to such children as "good adoptees" (p. 54). She said the "Good Adoptee . . . was placid, obedient, didn't ask too many questions, was sensitive to his [her] parent's needs to make believe he [she] wasn't adopted" (p. 54).

Family scapegoats often feel hurt, angry, and rejected. Sometimes they are hostile and aggressive. They tend to draw negative attention to themselves, and sometimes to their families. An adopted child says, "You're not my 'real' mother. You can't make me do that, because if you do I'll run away and find my 'real' parents." Lifton (1979) calls the family scapegoat "The Bad Adoptee" (p. 9). Some do poorly in school, get pregnant out of wedlock, abuse drugs, or engage in other socially unacceptable behavior. Family scapegoats come to the attention of and receive help from professionals that often see their problematic behaviors as indigenous to adopted children. It is probable that those adoptive children referred to guidance clinics, or psychiatric services that show, " . . . a rate of four percent of non-relative adoptions at such agencies as compared with an estimated rate of one percent of such children in the general population" (Kadushin, 1974, p. 603; Kadushin & Martin, 1988, p. 622) were functioning as family scapegoats.

The lost child may be quiet and shy, spend a lot of time alone, and escape conflict and stress by avoiding family interaction. "They are always in the background and never cause trouble" (Seixas & Youcha, 1985, p. 49). Their parents wonder why they never talk about adoption; or raise few if any questions. Lost children may be the brother or sister of a family scapegoat and often want to avoid causing their parent's additional pain.

Letting Go of Denial

Should problems arise, adoptive families tend to deny that adoption may be causal. "Denial is the common currency of troubled families" (Greenleaf, 1984, p. 9). Some time, perhaps in young adulthood, and often after a life cycle event like marriage, the birth of a child, or the death of a parent an adopted person begins to gain understandings and develop perspectives about what being adopted means to them. New feelings, based on past experiences, bring adult understandings. Emerging awareness and enlightenment mark the start of a process of letting go of denial. Boundaries between themselves and their adoptive families become clearer. Some may now acknowledge to themselves and others that they do belong to their birth families through heredity. "I'd really like to know something about my medical background." "I was just wondering if she was looking for me." There is often newfound support for these feelings and experiences. A spouse says, "I think she should know. I'd certainly want to know if I were adopted." Another says, "We're going to have our first child. I'd like to know more about his mother, so I told him I'd help him search."

Later in the process adopted persons begin to address some of the core issues and feelings associated with being adopted. Search represents a step in that process. For some adopted persons choosing to search means giving up some of the enabling behaviors that for them meant denying their needs, and taking responsibility for protecting their parents from the realities of adoptive parenthood. For adopted persons a search is the ultimate act of reality testing. A completed search may bring a sense of accomplishment. It represents taking control over what happened as a result of their adoption. For many search means getting in touch with painful, long denied, and sometimes surprising feelings of anger and loss. Finally, it is a time that adopted persons begin to trust their true feelings, become more fully sensitized to what being adopted means, and recognize their past experiences as being valid.

Integration marks the processes final phase. An adopted person may now come fully to terms with who they are. For the most part knowledge has replaced falsehoods and myths, ignorance, inconsistencies, confusion, and fantasy. Many find that reconnecting with their roots means newfound peace and satisfaction. There is a coming together of thoughts, feelings, expectations, and behaviors. Some begin a period of social activism directed toward undoing discriminatory adoption policies and laws. Most at this stage recognize that, " . . . There is no way to change one's ancestors, one's birth parents, or one's genes. The family into which one is born holds a unique place for each of us" (Watson, 1982, p. 15).

Implications for Practice

The traditional adoptive family represents a family variant that must co-exist within a culture that places inordinately high value on the dominant procreative family. Thus to varying degrees, children, parents, and professionals alike minimize, rationalize, or deny adoptive family differences. Nonetheless, adopted children come into their families through a social and legal process, not by birth, and with a genetic endowment unrelated to the parents that raise them. That difference singularly distinguishes them from procreative families.

As adoption became more institutionalized in the late 1930's-1940's, child welfare evolved a model that was intended to mirror the procreative family ideal. Policy required that states pass legislation obliterating the child's hereditary past. Adoption practice that once was less secret and more open now became protective, secretive, paternalistic, and closed. Child welfare denied, failed to recognize, and only recently acknowledged that adopted children grow up to become adopted adults, and that adoption is a lifelong process, not a single event. Family secrets now institutionalized through sealed birth records remain rigidly defended, protected, and maintained. But the primary emphasis on secrecy contributes to the denial of differences and distortions of reality.

Denial among professionals that are sometimes themselves adoptive family members include agency directors, adoption workers, attorneys and psychotherapists. Some fit the role of "professional enablers" in that they engage in co-dependent patterns of behavior like avoidance, covering up, denial of differences, protection, and taking responsibility for others that lead them to block change, and to maintain a dysfunctional system.

Denial of adoptive family differences indicates possible dysfunction within the adoptive family system. The specific characteristics that distinguish adoptive families from procreative families are those that adoptive family members are most likely to deny, and lead to co-dependent patterns of response, and the potential for adoptive family dysfunction. It is within the context of this complex and vulnerable family system that conflicts and issues arise. Yet, there is still a tendency to identify the child as the unit of treatment. Finally, there is need for empirical research to assess more fully the impact of the culture on adoptive family systems.

References

Andrews, R. G. (1979). A clinical appraisal of searching. *Public Welfare, 37, 3*, 15-21.

Co-dependency. An Emerging Issue. (1984). Pompano Beach, FL: Health Communications, Inc.

Greenleaf, J. (1984). Co-alcoholic/para-alcoholic: who's who and what's the difference? In *Co-dependency. An emerging issue.* Pompano Beach, FL: Health Communications, Inc.

Haase, T. (1977, March 31). Adoptees push right to records. *The Montgomery Journal.*

Hollenbach, W. L. (1973). No questions haunt me. *National Adoptalk, 9, 4,* pp. 1, 5.

Kadushin, A. (1974). *Child welfare services.* (2nd. ed.) New York: Macmillan Publishing Company.

Kadushin, A., & Martin, J. A. (1988). *Child welfare services.* (4th ed.). New York: Macmillan Publishing Company.

Lifton, B. J. (1979). *Lost and found. The adoption experience.* New York: The Dial Press.

Livingston, G. S. (1977, June). Search for a stranger. *Reader's Digest*, pp. 85-89.

Mississippi, State of. (1951, April). *Adoption survey.*

Satir, V. (1972). *People making.* Palo Alto: Science and Behavior Books.

Schwan, J., & Tuskan, M. (1979). The adoptive child. In J. Noshpitz, (Ed.) *Basic handbook of child psychiatry.* New York: Basic Books.

Seixas, J. S., & Youcha, G. (1985). *Children of alcoholism. A survivor's manual.* New York, NY: Harper & Row, Publishers.

Subby, R. & Friel, J. (1984). Co-dependency: A paradoxical dependency. In *Co-dependency. An emerging issue.* Pompano Beach, FL: Health Communications, Inc.

The Child and The State. Vol. 1. (1938). Chicago: University of Chicago Press.

Toussieng, P. W. (1962). Thoughts regarding the etiology of psychological difficulties in adopted children. *Child Welfare, 41,* 59-65.

Watson, K. (1982). A bold new model for foster family care. *Public Welfare, 40, 2,* p. 15.

Wegscheider-Cruse, S. (1984). Co-dependency: The therapeutic void. In *Co-dependency. An emerging issue.* Pompano Beach, FL: Health Communications, Inc.

White, R. B., & Gilliland, R. M. (1978). *Elements of psychopathology. The mechanisms of defense.* New York: Grune & Stratton.

Whitfield, C. (1984). Co-dependency: An emerging problem among professionals. In *Co-dependency. An emerging issue.* Pompano Beach, FL: Health Communications, Inc.

Woititz, J. G. (1983). *Adult children of alcoholics.* Pompano Beach, FL: Health Communications, Inc.

The Task of Telling

Good adoption practice for years promoted the idea that it was better for parents to tell their children that they were adopted. Not telling was discouraged. Workers encouraged generations of adoptive parents to read their children a little book by Valentina Wasson (1939). This story introduced the "chosen child" myth. Parents explained that the child's birthmother could not keep the child. But she loved the child so much she, "gave her child away" to be adopted. Mommy and Daddy, "couldn't have children of their own," so they adopted a child. No doubt these rationalizations, apologies, euphemisms, and myths were well intended. Nonetheless, their underlying messages are emotionally unhealthy, non-constructive, and negative. They fostered unrealistic expectations. They placed undue burdens on adoptive parents and children. They are still at the root of many clinical issues in working with adoptive families today

Issues About Telling

What, when, how and whether to tell a child that he or she is adopted is still a significant topic of interest and concern at pre and post-adoptive parent groups, adoption seminars, and in adoption books. Adoption specialists, mental health professionals, and adoptive parents generate diverse opinions and theories. Some advocate never telling the child. Others suggest telling the child at various ages and developmental stages (Lawton & Gross, 1964, Kadushin, 1974, Kadushin & Martin, 1988). The task of telling is not simple. It brings out the many complex issues faced by adoptive family members. Telling, " . . . forces both adoptive parent and child into an explicit recognition of their adoptive status" (Kadushin, 1974, p. 547). It is where adoption mythology, attitudes, beliefs, and feelings conflict. It is adoption in a microcosm.

People need a positive, constructive, and empowering approach to the task of telling. One grounded in reality, and not fantasy. But first, do we know why the telling task is an object of dread and a subject for debate? Do people still perceive the telling message as something hurtful, damaging, shameful, and stigmatizing? Could we, however unintentionally, be perpetuating our own negative adoption attitudes, prejudices, misperceptions, and associations?

Anxieties About Telling

The difficulties we have with finding the "right way" to inform children of their adoptive status lie within ourselves. They stem directly from our personal perceptions of adoption. For most of us, these perceptions are both positive and negative. The telling task stimulates anxieties about our negative perceptions. If people believed that telling children they are adopted would be perceived as good news, the difficulty with what to say, when and how to say it would be obviated. People want to shout good news from the rooftops. But when people are confronted with the telling task, they are forced to face an unpleasant truth. Within our social milieu, many hold negative adoption attitudes, prejudices, misperceptions, and associations. Most of us hold some of these ourselves. We know from personal experience that they exist in others. Many of us experience powerful feelings about adoption that range from joyousness to shame.

The Pain of Telling

The task of telling customarily falls to the parents. Often how each feels about his or her adoptive parent status determines how, what, when and who tells. The road leading to adoption can be long, complicated, frustrating, and painful. Many that struggle to conceive a child feel demeaned, diminished, and disempowered when they fail. In *The Baby Chase*, Washington Post sports columnist Tony Kornheiser (1983) says:

> I want to tell you what it feels like not to be able to have a kid, what it does to your self-esteem and your self-image, not to mention your sex life. What it does to you psychologically, emotionally . . . spiritually . . . . Day after day, month after month, year after year . . . to suffer such profound pain . . . . Why can't we make a baby? What did we do that was so terrible, so awful? (pp. 4-5).

An adoptive mother says:

> A year or so ago, the idea of a birthmother was so threatening to me. It was just some terrible obstacle between me and getting a baby. At that point, I didn't want to deal with birthmothers at all. I wanted my own baby. And if I couldn't have that, I wanted the closest thing I could get to it. (Siegel, 1993, p. 17).

Many continue to grieve their losses. Thoughts about having to tell, and the telling process can aggravate their feelings.

The telling task forces parents to face issues and feelings about being different. A recent survey of American attitudes toward adoption (Lewin,

1997) indicates that, " . . . although most people support the concept of adoption, they have questions about the experience of children and parents who participate in this profound alteration of biological family relationships" (Downs, Moore, McFadden, & Costin, 2000, p. 384). "Telling makes explicit the fact of infertility; telling introduces the [birth] parent's image into the family system and threatens the exclusiveness of the relationship between adoptive parents and child" (Kadushin & Martin, 1988, p. 575). But some adoptive parents, that place a high value on not being different, often trivialize and deny these differences. So that however outwardly the adoptive family appears like a non-adoptive family, the task of telling brings home a reality. This family is formed differently that most other families. A social and legal process forms this family, not a birth process.

Delay Telling?

Some psychiatrists (Schechter, 1960, Peller, 1961) suggest that parents delay telling because theoretically the child might suffer a "severe narcissistic injury" (Schechter, 1960, p. 31). They caution that parents should wait until the child is old enough to better "handle" the message, so that the child's ego strength is considered at different developmental stages. The concept of a deep narcissistic injury might apply to adoptive parents with equal force. Adoptive children and parents face self-esteem issues associated with infertility, illegitimacy, and minority family status. Enhancing self-esteem is a challenge for both. Adoption is a lifelong experience. Gaining insights and understandings is a lifelong process. The message, for the child, gains in significance over the years.

Not Telling?

Adoptive parents that are deeply into denial are not likely to tell at all. Others may delay the process interminably. They become caught up in a troublesome quest, never feeling they have found the right words, or the right time. For some parents it is like telling children about sex. They tell quickly, without discussion, and only once. Those that do not or will not tell risk the likely probability that someone else will. A neighbor's child. An aunt or cousin. Keeping the adoption a secret, or withholding significant information from the child can foster a "family secret" pathology. Family therapist Virginia Satir (1972) says, "fear and shame are usually the basis for most family secrets, which most often are rationalized as protection of the kids" (p. 107). Children that discover that their parents have failed to tell them about their adoption may feel that their parents cannot be trusted about other matters of importance. Not telling—or telling in a hurried and self-conscious way—tells the child that adoptive status is bad. That it is so bad it is not a topic for discussion. It is a short jump from understanding that message to the child concluding that there must be something bad about him or her, as well.

Going About Telling

So how do we go about the telling task? Let us explore using a more positive, less damaging, more constructive, less negative, and more truthful approach. We know that for the child telling begins a process of understanding. Many questions are likely to arise. Let us accept that we may not have answers. Often we really do not know why or how the birthparent's choice was made. We may only believe we know. It is O.K. to say, "I don't know." What we can say with certainty is, "She, he or they made a choice." Sometimes we rush to answers in the hope that we can make it all right, or make it go away. Often when we do that, we lose an important opportunity to ask the child what he or she is thinking. Let the child tell us how he or she sees it. Be willing to listen actively to the child's concerns. Learning to use empowering, affirming, enhancing and constructive adoptive family communication skills is inherently worthwhile.

Adoption Happens to Parent and Child

Begin by recognizing that adoption is something that happens to both parent and child. Traditionally we have singled out the child as though adoption only happens to him or her. That approach falsely and mistakenly placed the onus on the child. In fact, adoption is a process that is solely initiated by adults—those that seek children in need of parenting, and those that are unable or unwilling to parent the child they conceive. The responsibility lies squarely with the adults—never with the child.

Not Laying the Burden on the Child

Adoptive parents, birth parents, and adoptive children have dissimilar issues to resolve. Laying parental issues on the child is wrong. However they came to adoption it was the parent's choice to adopt or relinquish. Placing the burden for their decision(s) on the child can never be rightfully justified. Moreover, in the past parents tried to explain away the child's issues—rejection, abandonment, loss, being different, and the stigma of illegitimacy—by talking about their own issues. "Mommy and daddy could not have children of their own." "She was too young." Adoptive parents may feel a compelling need to protect their children. But these issues remain the child's to work out over time.

"You" Messages and "We" Messages

Consider eliminating "you" messages when telling, or talking about adoption. You messages have traditionally communicated adoptive family differences. "There is something mommy and daddy have to tell you." "Mommy and Daddy didn't give birth to you. You were adopted." "Your birth mother loved you so much she gave you away to be adopted." "Mommy and Daddy adopted you because we couldn't have any children of our own." "No you weren't born at ——— hospital, like Johnny. We adopted you." You messages mistakenly imply that adoption only happens to the child. Instead, begin to use "we" messages when telling, or talking about adoption. We messages appropriately signal the fact that adoption is something that happens to both parents and children. We messages no longer single out the child as though adoption only happened to them. We messages shift the emphasis away from the child's status, toward the family's status, where it fittingly belongs. There is, however, a caveat. Some parents—that have not yet found a way to let go of past issues—may be unwilling or unable to move beyond their perception that adoption is at best—still only second best. They may find themselves stuck in the past, and see adoption only in terms of you messages. They may need to work through their disappointment, shame, and grief

Adoption is a Shared Experience

So how do we tell a child that he or she was adopted? Recognize that adoption does not happen only to the child. It fact it never did. Adoption is a shared experience that begins with parents—those that seek children in need of someone to parent them, and those that cannot or will not parent the children they bear. Parents that for whatever the reasons ultimately choose to adopt can tell the child, "We are an adoptive family."

References

Downs, S. W., Moore, E., McFadden, E. J., & Costin, L. B. (2000). *Child welfare and family services* (6th ed.). Boston: Allyn & Bacon.

Kadushin, A. (1974). *Child welfare services.* (2nd. ed.). New York: Macmillan Publishing Company.

Kadushin, A., & Martin, J. A. (1988). *Child welfare services.* (4th ed.). New York: Macmillan Publishing Company.

Kornheiser, T. (1983). *The baby chase.* New York: Macmillan Publishing Company.

Lawton, J. L., & Gross, S. Z. (1964). Review of psychiatric literature on adopted children. *Archives of general psychiatry. 11,* 633-644.

Lewin, T. (1997, November 9). U. S. is divided on adoption, survey of attitudes asserts. *New York Times*, p. 10.

Peller, L. (1961). About "telling the child" about his adoption. *Bulletin of the Philadelphia Association for Psychoanalysts, 11,* 145-154.

Schechter, M. D. (1960, July). Observation on adopted children. *A.M. A. Archives of general psychiatry, 3, 21-32.*

Siegel, D. H. (1993). Open adoption of infants: Adoptive parent's perceptions of advantages and disadvantages. *Social Work. 38, 1, 15-23.*

Wasson, V. P. (1939). *The chosen baby.* New York: Carrick and Evans.

Clinical Notes

Adoption may directly affect as many as one out of eight American families. There are no reliable statistics about the number of adopted children or adults in the United States (Downs, Moore, McFadden, & Costin, 2000, p. 400). Estimates range from five to nine million. The lower bound estimate of five million is 2.5 percent of the total population (Gallagher & Rajsock, U. S. Children's Bureau, Department of Health, Education, and Welfare, personal communication, March, 1975). For every adopted person count at least one adoptive parent and two birth parents plus additional siblings, grandparents and other extended kinship. Adopted children that have a genetic endowment unrelated to that of the parents that raise them are the subject of this paper.

Nineteen hundred and seventy marked a peak year for white, non-relative, infant adoptions in the U.S. (Statistical Abstract of, 1972, p. 305). These adopted persons are now entering their thirties, a time when people experience life cycle events like marriage, the birth of a child, or the loss of a parent. This statistic increases the likelihood that more adopted persons will show up in clinical practices. Adopted persons seek help for the same reasons as anyone else. Still, Anderson (1993) suggests that everyone start with the assumption " . . . that adoption plays a big role in the life of every adoptee" (p. 160). And Hartman and Laird (1990) urge clinicians to recognize, explore, and assess adoption's salience " . . . even though it may seem remote to the issue at hand," and adoptive family members deny its " . . . importance or relevance" (p. 228).

Being Adopted

Abandonment, rejection, identity, illegitimacy, bastardy, and the image of the "bad seed" are issues that relate to being adopted. They remain with adopted persons throughout their lives. Adopted persons begin coping with them from the moment they know that they came into their families through adoption. They are universal to adopted persons whether the adoption was open or closed, they were infants or older, or came from a foreign country. They become part of how adopted persons identify themselves, and how other people identify adopted persons. Any one of these issues may be worthy of therapeutic consideration.

Effects of Social and Cultural Factors

A number of social and cultural factors that have influenced American adoption policy and practice have exerted a profound effect on adopted persons and adoptive families.

First, an historical affinity between social casework and psychodynamic theory led to the use of a medical model to understand adoption; an intense interest in early object relations, prolongation of the family romance fantasy, and the intra-psychic life of the adopted child; and the notion that disturbances in genealogical bewilderment be defined as symptoms of adopted child pathology.

Second, child welfare policies that value confidentiality and protection, and adoption practices that were designed to deny that there are differences between adoptive and procreative families made it difficult, if not impossible to obtain data. What there is has mostly come second hand from the observations of adoptive parents, adoption workers, and clinicians.

Third, much of adoption practice was based on social attitudes and values originated in the context of society sixty years ago. In an attempt to effect a "clean break" between the child, their hereditary history and genetic origins, traditional adoption practice has mandated sealed birth and adoption records since the late 1930's.

Fourth, adoptive family members have to cope with negative societal attitudes and adoptive family minority status. In an article on "The Adoptive Child" from *The Basic Handbook of Child Psychiatry* (1979) Schwan and Tuskan say, "Society tends to condemn adoption" (p. 345).

Fifth, adoption practice developed without benefit of family theory. Hence, differences in adoptive family structure, the parent's adjustment to adoption, and infertility, the adoptive child-parent bond, the search, and the role of the birth family, have not been fully addressed in terms of family theory and clinical practice, by contrast to the attention devoted to the adopted child's intra-psychic life.

Sixth, myth has played a powerful and enduring role in adoption practice. The fundamental adoption myth is that there are no differences between adoptive families and non-adoptive families. The myth functions to convey the notion that adopted children have no existence prior to adoption, and are neither conceived, nor born, and therefore have no ancestry, no genetic history, and no past. The myth fosters unrealistic expectations among adoptive parents and their children.

Seventh, if no differences exist between adoptive and non-adoptive families then it follows that there should be no special problems related to adoption. In the event that a problem does arise, it follows that the problem would have to be indigenous to the child.

Eighth, the feelings, attitudes, and behaviors of adoptive family members are often inconsistent with the expectations underlying traditional adoption practice.

Dysfunctional Outcomes

Boszormenyi-Nagy (1973) contends that an early adoption can seem to create a situation psychologically equal to procreative parenting. But the situation is more complex. Secrets about birth parents, and the protection of the adoptive family all have inherent denial characteristics. Adoptive parents, " . . . appear as usurping undeservedly exclusive rights . . . . Ties of blood thus may be the stronger . . . " (p. 113). Adoptive parents must resolve, " . . . the ambiguity between their initial certainty of their rights and commitment to parenthood . . . and the fact of not having provided such biological ministrations" (p. 133).

The ghost-like, shadowy presence of the child's birth parent may handicap the development of the parent subsystem. Freedman, Kaplan, and Saddock (1976) suggest, " . . . a family may be skewed when a dyad other than the parental one dominates the group emotionally . . . " (p. 183).

Goldstein, Freud, and Solnit (1977) say:

> The psychological parent-child relationship remains incomplete if it is emotionally one-sided. That the parent is an essential figure for the child's feelings needs to be complemented by the child's figuring in a similar way in the parent's emotional life (p. 20).

Yet, in some adoptive families the psychological parent-child bond may remain forever tentative. The complementary state proposed by Goldstein, Freud, and Solnit may never be achieved. The parents may ultimately fail to accept a child born to other parents as their "psychological child."

The extent to which any one individual believes in, adheres to, or values the fundamental adoption myth, or any part of it, or any derivative from it depends on how well it serves that particular individual. That individual may be an adoptive family member, an adoption industry worker, an adoption professional, or a psychotherapist treating adoptive parents or children. Nonetheless, the child's heredity cannot be eliminated. Moreover, the primary emphasis on secrecy contributes to the denial of differences and distortions of reality.

The strength with which individuals adhere to this myth, in total or in part, and the denial that accompanies it, lies at the root of many clinical issues that arise in working with adoptive family members. Clinicians place a high value on awareness of personal biases, prejudices, values, and beliefs. Keeping this goal in mind, let's look at some of the objective differences and the similarities between adoptive and non-adoptive families.

Adoption Realities

- An adopted child is a child first—adoption happens second.

- Like all other children, adopted persons are conceived by a man and a woman, and come into being through a birth process.

- Like all other children, adopted children share a common genetic ancestry with and have blood ties to their birth parents.

- There is no way for adopted children to share a common ancestry or have blood ties with their adoptive parents.

Still, many adoptive children and their parents minimize, trivialize, or deny these differences. For adopted persons adoption always means a loss of relationship with emotionally significant objects, and both a symbolic and an actual loss of their roots, as in their genetic identity and their ancestry, and a sense of connectedness. Becoming disconnected from one's ancestry is perhaps the loneliest experience known. It is like floating in time and space without an anchor. It means not belonging in a way that all others belong. Ironically, the child's sense of loneliness is felt even more when safely held within the loving bosom of their adoptive families. Perhaps a diluted version of this experience would be for non-adopted persons to think of how it feels and what it means to experience the sensation of feeling lonely in a crowd.

With each loss comes a need to grieve, and to work through the pain. Yet, both adoptive parents and children often lack that opportunity because these losses tend to go unrecognized by themselves and others. How adoptive family members perceive their differences, or whether they may in whole or in part deny them can be the basis for exploration with an adoptive person in therapy. The process by which these differences are denied provides a basis for adoptive family dysfunction.

For example, when an adoptive parent has invested in the fundamental adoption myth, the adopted child's basic sense of self has to develop around a faulty belief system—that there is no difference between being born to one's parents or being adopted by them. To maintain the fiction members of adoptive families learn to develop patterns of behavior, including special language and methods of problem solving that are grounded in denial and maintained by a set of unspoken and unwritten rules.

Maintaining the Myth

- The child's past, or the child's illegitimate status, or the fact of the adoption itself, or any other adoption related differences may be perceived by the adoptive family as deficits the family ought to try to overcome.

- The family may decide to cope with this problem by trying to hide the fact that they are an adoptive family.

- Communications related to the adoption become limited or non-existent, tend to be faulty, confusing, inconsistent and emotional, and often reflect a denial of the adoption.

- Family members may have difficulty identifying or expressing any feelings about adoption.

- Fantasies replace reality.

- Attitudes and beliefs related to adoption tend to become rigid.

- Family members may experience feelings of powerlessness, as in not having been able to make choices. Some may feel like they have to make up for something missing in the family, or feel that they are responsible for the feelings or behaviors of other family members. Others share a basic sense of shame or low self-esteem, and a strong need for approval from within the family, or in the social system.

The Adoptee as Scapegoat

Family theory identifies faulty communications, low self-esteem, minority status, and family structure as factors that may contribute to family dysfunction. At some point in the adoptive family life cycle an adoptive family that structured itself as though it were a non-adoptive family may become dysfunctional. The child with his unknown and hidden past becomes an easy scapegoat, "the symptom bearer." Family therapists Minuchin and Fishman (1981) say, "Symptoms are as likely or more likely to be the result of stresses in the family organism. The relationship of the symptom to the family organism should be assessed" (p. 56).

The Unit of Treatment

A family therapy approach emphasizes the family as the unit of treatment. Friedman, et al. (1976) say, "It is not that there is a patient with something wrong—but that symptomatic behavior is a contract between two or more people" (p. 923). Sherman (1974) says:

> When the family therapist approaches the problem of an individual person, he [she] always respects the individuality of the problem and of the pain; and he [she] also interprets them as symptomatic expressions of a problem, a distortion, a disability in the family . . . (p. 460).

Coping with Adoption

How do adopted persons learn to cope with adoption? Some discover that it may be safer not to share their feelings, fears, worries, or hurts. They learn how to discount and repress their feelings. Others come to deny that they have any thoughts and feelings about adoption. They learn to trivialize, minimize and deny that there are any differences in adoption. Some, that lack validation for their experiences, learn to mistrust their sense of what is real.

Adopted persons tend to be very loyal to their adoptive parents. Most will say that their parents are the mother and father that raised them. Many engage in enabling behaviors that protect their parents, especially if they perceive that their parents are uncomfortable with their adoptive family status.

Consequences

Minuchin says families frame their reality according to their own idiosyncratic definition of truth, and then label their experiences in ways "appropriate" to fit the "family truth" (Minuchin & Fishman, 1981). In a similar way, child welfare has conceptualized the child as an entity independent of birth family context. Traditional adoption practice has institutionalized this idiosyncratic definition of child to fit practice "truth." Professionals that support this idiosyncratic definition of truth may serve to maintain a dysfunctional system.

Adoption profoundly influences those that it touches, though there are social and cultural factors that work against recognition of this reality. Many adoptive family members will deny its importance. Clinicians need to be aware of the possibility that they themselves may assume a co-dependent role. When adoption comes up in therapy, consider applying all of the usual and customary theoretical models that clinicians already know and use. The fact that the problem appears to be associated with adoption is neither the time nor the reason to suspend a clinician's usual and customary knowledge base.

References

Anderson, R. (1993). *Second choice.* Growing up adopted. Chesterfield, MO: Badger Hill Press.

Boszormenyi-Nagy, I., & Spark, G. (1973). *Invisible loyalties.* Hagerstown, MD: Harper & Row, Publishers.

Downs, S. W., Moore, E., McFadden, E. J., & Costin, L. B. (2000). *Child welfare and family services* (6th ed.). Boston: Allyn & Bacon.

Freedman, A. M., Kaplan, H. C., & Saddock, B. J. (1976). *Modern synopsis of comprehensive textbook of psychiatry II.* (2nd ed.). Baltimore: Williams & Wilkins, Co.

Goldstein, J., Freud, A., & Solnit, A. J. (1973). *Beyond the best interests of the child.* New York: The Free Press.

Hartman, A., & Laird, J. (1990). Family treatment after adoption. In D. M. Brodzinsky & M. D. Schechter, (Eds.) *The psychology of adoption* (pp. 221-239). New York: Oxford University Press.

Minuchin, S., & Fishman, H. C. (1981). F*amily therapy techniques.* Cambridge: Harvard University Press.

Satir, V. (1972). *People making.* Palo Alto, CA: Science and Behavior Books, Inc.

Schwan, J., & Tuskan, M. (1979). The adoptive child. In Joseph Noshpitz, (Ed.), *Basic handbook of child psychiatry.* New York: Basic Books, Inc.

Sherman, S. N. (1974). Family therapy. In F. J. Turner, (Ed.), *Social work treatment* (pp. 457-489). New York: The Free Press.

Statistical Abstract of the United States. (1972). U. S. Government Printing Office: Washington, DC.

Discrimination Against the Adoptee

In the next five years an estimated one half million children adopted in the United States will attain a majority (U. M. Gallagher, & A. Rajsock, The Children's Bureau, U. S. Department of Health, Education, and Welfare, personal communication, March, 1975). At that time, they will have achieved the right to vote, to marry without parental consent, and to enter into contracts. They will have attained full adult status in every respect but one. Sanctioned by American adoption policy and law—intended to protect them as children—these adults remain deprived of the right to direct access to information concerning their genetic heritage, their ethnicity, their biological parentage, and their birth name. The scope for this policy extends to almost every adopted child or adult, whether adopted as infants or older, or by relatives or non-relatives.

In the 1940's, states began enacting legislation designed to keep information about an adopted person's birth origins confidential. So birth and adoption records were sealed. "Amended" birth certificates—that substituted the names of the adoptive parents for the names of the birth parents—were issued. The new certificate became the only proof of birth available for public inspection. Access to the original birth certificate could be gained only by court order and for "good cause." But such court orders are rarely granted. Courts are reluctant not to follow legislatively established mandates (Folkenberg, Harrington, & Saba, 1979). The sealed record laws were made to apply retroactively in some states.

The rationale behind sealed record laws was to remove the "stigma of illegitimacy" from the public record. Undoubtedly, most children adopted before World War II were born out of wedlock. Yet, before the 1940's there was no sealed record policy. The sealing of birth and adoption records is a relatively recent phenomenon. Adopted persons that are now in their thirties represent the first generation to have had their birth records sealed at adoption.

A 1977 study indicates that sealed record laws have been effective. Of those adult adoptees surveyed, a sample possessed virtually no information concerning their genetic origins. Adult adopted persons reported that they knew an average of three out of twenty-two items of information concerning their national, ethnic, and religious backgrounds, as well as the physical, occupational, health, educational, or personality characteristics of their genetic forebears. It was clear that the question, "Who am I?" could not be answered by adoptees in terms of their "genetic identity" (Small, p. 54).

The rationale underlying the enactment of sealed record legislation is increasingly being called into question. Still, most state legislatures refuse to make amends. When open record legislation was enacted in Minnesota in 1978, the principle of restoring the right of adult adopted citizens to direct access to their original birth record at majority was compromised. The adult adopted person's birthparents were granted an ascendant right to a veto. Such a restriction is analogous to compromising a citizen's right to vote by requiring them to pay a poll tax or pass a literacy test.

Discrimination is defined as making a distinction " . . . in favor of or against a person . . . on the basis of the group, class, or category to which the person . . . belongs, rather than according to actual merit" (Stein, 1967, p. 411). Adult adopted persons are the victims of such discrimination. In all but seven states adult adopted citizens are currently denied access to their original birth record, and, consequently, to knowledge of their genetic origins when all other citizens have that right. That is discrimination.

The estimated five million adopted persons in the United States comprise a minority, a " . . . social group in some way distinct from the dominant, more influential group in the society" (Dressler, 1969, p. 516). It is the fact of having been adopted, of having become members of a family through a legal rather than a biological process, that distinguishes adopted persons from the dominant, nonadopted population. Membership in this minority is usually not a matter of choice. It is customarily attained by means of a legal process in which the adopted person has had no voice.

Why Adopted Persons Choose to Remain Closeted

Adopted persons are not visible as members of a minority group. Their adoptive status sets them apart. They are stigmatized by negative attitudes toward illegitimacy whether they were born out of wedlock or not. The media has contributed substantially to raising public consciousness concerning matters of adoption within the last few years. There have been stories about adoption custody cases, legislation to open records, the adoption reform movement, and adoptees in search of their roots. And dramatizations like the television series Roots and the movie Superman that highlight matters of identity. Still, the vast majority of adopted persons choose to remain closeted. The following examples may tell why.

An editor and married father of three discovered at age forty-six that he had been adopted in infancy. He reacted with feelings of shock, anger, disbelief, and disconnectedness. He said, "The news hit me harder than anything . . . I found out my birth certificate was a fraud . . . I felt it imperative that I find out my origins" (Haase, 1977). He had read an article, "Adoptees: Opening Doors to the Past or a Pandora's Box?" in The Washington Post a month before (White, 1975). Now the article took on new importance. When he chose to tell a few close friends about his unhappy discovery, or that his newly found adoptive status resulted from the momentary slip of an elderly aunt's tongue their reaction took him by surprise. "Oh, gee, what a shock. Well, look, it's really OK . . . That is . . . we mean . . . we still like you."

Before a broadcast on the subject of adoption, a Takoma Park, Maryland radio announcer confessed to an adopted guest that as a child, the cruelest, most devastating, worst possible thing that he could think to do to get even with his sister was to tell her that she was adopted, though he knew in fact that was not the case.

Adoptive mother and child psychologist Eda LeShan suggests that adoptees that search appear to lack impulse control, not unlike thieves. In the March, 1977 issue of Woman's Day magazine she said:

> . . . I am deeply concerned about [adoptees] who search for their biological roots. I am not bothered by the fact that they want to . . . but that they give in to this impulse . . . . We are almost constantly bombarded by impulses to which we must learn not to give in! . . . . Times when we'd like to hit someone . . . times when we'd love to steal . . . .

Maturity comes when we learn to control such impulses
. . . . It seems to me that in most circumstances it's [search]
an impulse that needs to be controlled (p. 40).

In Public Affairs Pamphlet No. 274 (1974) LeShan says, "Every state has laws requiring that a court order must be obtained in order for adoption records to be seen, and this is granted only under the most unusual or special circumstances" (p. 1). Adoptive parents should accept their child's momentary curiosity but " . . . not permit those feelings to lead to action . . . as a search is unrealistic and can lead to unhappiness and disillusionment" (p. 26).

A social work colleague that was adopted through a Catholic agency asked them for non-identifying family background information. She found herself subjected to a one and one-half hour interview. Sensitive to the nature of the agency's line of questioning she asked the worker, "Are you giving me a mental status exam"? "I would if I could," the worker answered.

Adoptive parent and state senator Victor Crawford (1979) testifying against Senate Bill No. 837 before a Maryland Senate Judicial Proceedings Committee motioned toward a group of adopted persons there to testify as proponents of open record legislation. Crawford declared that adoptees had sordid origins; that a number of these "kids" were " . . . born as a result of incest, murder, rape, and robbery;" and that the damage done by opening records could be "astronomical." Another senator testified that there could be no question that where babies were given up for adoption, some of the facts are very grim, and that there can be no excuse for disrupting a family years later by resurrecting the grim facts.

The prior year Elizabeth Baker, an attorney with Legal Aid in Baltimore, Maryland testified before a House Judiciary proceedings committee that records ought not to be opened to adult adopted persons. Baker said, "It is not a rosy situation when someone's being placed for adoption. There may be rape or incest involved, or the mother may have been . . . an inmate of some institution" (Barringer, 1978, p. A 1).

Baker cited a story about a 23-year-old adopted person that had recently:

> . . . asked a judge to unseal the records of his birth. Shortly before he made a decision on the request, the judge was told by a psychiatrist that the youth was a psychopath who was seeking his natural mother in order to murder her (Barringer, 1978, p. A 12, col. 1).

A Washington Star (1978) editorial opined that:

> . . . placing a child for adoption seldom, if ever, is a matter that does not involve grievous personal burdens, guilts, [and] apprehensions. Having made so momentous and painful a decision, ought [birthmothers] not be shielded from again having to confront that terrible circumstance in the future? ("Adoptees and balancing equities," p. A)

Responding to an article "Who Am I?" (Wright, 1978) in *The Washington Post Magazine,* Michael Bentzen (1978), an adoptive father and president of the Barker Foundation, a private DC adoption agency wrote:

> Adult adoptees . . . become incensed when someone suggests that satisfaction of their normal curiosity about their birth parents is not . . . among other things, their "birthright" (p. 66).

An aspect of the article which is startling is Wright's suggestion that searching adoptees would not harm biological parents . . . [and] will exercise discretion to avoid embarrassing or harming [them] . . . . Of course Wright did not mention . . . the February 3, 1978 Post article wherein the motive of an adoptee to find his biological mother was to kill her . . . (p. 66).

I am opposed to efforts to change the laws of the District of Columbia and Maryland to open adoption records to young persons of 18 and 21 years of age without minimal safeguards, such as screening the motives of the adoptees . . . . Giving a hunting license . . . usually portends ill for the quarry (p. 66).

On the op Ed page of The Washington Post (1979) adoptive mother and DC City Council member Willie J. Hardy wrote that the DC "Inspection of Adoptee's Records Act of 1979" was:

. . . lopsided to the pinnacle of selfishness . . . .

The precedent of unsealing records would be a dangerous one . . . .

A small minority within the minority of this city's population seeks questionable privileges . . . "questionable" because their motives are suspect . . . .

The paramount dangerous legal precedent this bill would establish is to allow any adopted person access to adoption records regardless of the date or time of adoption . . . That would cause serious traumatic experiences for . . . thousands of birth parents and adoptive parents . . . .

This is regardless of whether the adoptee has an emotional or mental illness propelling him [or her] to seek the birth parent(s) for all the wrong reasons . . . .

> The selfishness of this bill is blatantly horrible . . . .
> Recognize this bill for what it is: legislation to give a small
> group of people with selfish interests what they want—
> whatever that is (p. A19).

Maryland State senator Victor Crawford and DC city council member Willie J. Hardy are credited with leading the opposition that killed open record legislation in those jurisdictions. Legislators report that adoptive parents that registered their opposition to open record legislation frequently cite the privacy of the birth parent as their basis of concern.

In most states adults adopted as children remain forever children in terms of adoption law and practice. During deliberations over the "Inspection of Adoptee's Records Act of 1979" the DC City Council discussed raising the age of majority for adopted citizens from 18 to 21, to 25, to 35. Council members proposed that permission be obtained from both the adoptive parents and the birth parents before adopted persons of any age could view their original birth record, and suggested that adopted citizens seeking birth records from DC must be in need of psychological counseling. The messages communicated are blatantly discriminatory. They raise the question as to whether society is safe with adopted persons on the loose.

The Roots of Attitudes Toward Adopted Persons

The forgoing examples reflect the views of legislators, attorneys, adoptive parents, a psychologist, an adoption social worker, a media person, and others. They represent widely held negative, hostile, and punitive attitudes toward adopted persons. Hewitt and Pinchbeck (1969) suggest these attitudes may spring from deeply held religious, sexual, economic, and social values that have their roots in sixteenth century England.

> Until the sixteenth century, bastardy had not been thought of as any great shame. Men took care of their bastards, were indeed often proud of them, and in many cases brought them home to their wives or mothers to be brought up. Children born out of wedlock were thus found to be growing up in their father's house with their half-brothers and sisters without a hint of disgrace either to themselves or to their natural parents (p. 301).

The Poor Law of 1576 indicates a shift in attitude:

> First, concerning Bastards begotten and born out of lawful Matrimony (an Offence against Gods law and Mans Lawe) the said bastards now lefte to be kepte at the chardge of the Parishe where they bee borne, to the greate Burden of the same Parishe and in defrauding of the Reliefe of the impotent and aged true Poor of the same Parishe, and to the evil Example and Encouradgement of lewde Lyef . . . (pp. 206-220).

The association of adoption with illegitimacy is not without substance. Illegitimate children are the principal source for adoption by parents to whom they are not biologically related. The Children's Bureau, U. S. Department of Health, Education, and Welfare estimates that in the early 1970s illegitimate children accounted for 87 % of all non-relative adoptions (Kadushin, 1974). The circumstances surrounding the child's conception and relinquishment are deemed so undesirable that knowledge about them must be locked away for all time. But the societally sanctioned sealing of birth and adoption records perpetuates discrimination against adopted persons. Even the presumption that adopted persons must be protected from this information reinforces "bad seed" stereotypes. The sealed record policy generates and reinforces a public prejudice that is extremely resistant to modification or eradication.

The association of adoption with swearwords and shame exemplifies existing prejudice. Recently a syndicated columnist wrote, "The image of the unwed father was always a seedy one. He was a man who skipped town one step ahead of the shotgun. He left behind a woman 'in trouble,' and a child who grew up a swearword" (Goodman, 1979, p. A.15.). Another said, "Many of the children given up for adoption are illegitimate, and many more are born to teenage mothers ill-equipped to care for them." These mothers " . . . should have a chance to build a new life without remaining vulnerable to possible embarrassment and recrimination," and " . . . may not care to be confronted with [their] shame decades later" (Means, 1978).

Adopted Persons Are Stigmatized As Being Different, and Inferior

Arguments that deny an adult adopted citizen direct access to his or her original birth record—arguments that attest to the need for confidentiality or protection, freedom from the shame of illegitimacy, and questionable origins, etc.—become rationalizations in defense of discrimination. Adoptees become identified with a group that is stigmatized as being different, and inferior. Paradoxically, the primary recipient of adoption services, the child qua individual that the adoption establishment exists to serve—becomes an adversary when asking for that which is granted to all nonadopted persons.

The state, acting on the principle of parens patriae, is obligated to protect children through the exercise of legislative and regulatory powers like those embodied in adoption statutes and regulations (Kadushin, 1974). Statutes providing for the issuance of amended birth certificates and the sealing of the original birth record were based on recommendations of adoption workers. These recommendations provided the basis for the standards set by the Child Welfare League of America in 1938 (Folkenberg, Harrington, & Saba, 1979). Adoption practice and legislation have failed to take account of the fact that adopted children grow up.

Harriet Fricke, a University of Chicago School of Social Service graduate, and adoption caseworker and administrator for 20 years, left the child welfare field. Fricke said she could no longer go along with " . . . false birth certificates, burying the biological past . . . violating a child's civil rights" (Wilson, 1971). The adoption agencies gave all kinds of reasons why the sealed record policy was in effect. They talked about their commitment to the natural mother and to the adoptive parents, but " . . . nobody spoke about commitments to the child" (Wilson, 1971).

The adoption establishment is constituted by the courts and social service agencies that represent the state in carrying out their protective roles through child welfare services, special interests, such as adoption lobby groups like The National Council for Adoption (NCFA), private agencies like the Edna Gladney Home and the Barker Foundation, and attorneys specializing in family and adoption law. Those that work for the adoption industry seem especially threatened by suggestions, criticisms, and demands for reform from those that must live within the adoption system.

Adoption agency representatives and special interests subgroups argue that release of birth records to adult adopted persons would increase abortions and decrease adoptions. These arguments, unsubstantiated in Kansas and Alaska, that have open records, appear directed toward maintenance of personal and or institutional livelihood.

Adopted persons are the product of an industry that bestows special rights on adoptive and birth parent clients—and in the process, abrogates the rights of adopted persons to their original birth record. Arguments that deny adult adopted citizens direct access to their original birth records—like protection of birth and adoptive parents, and confidentiality—protect the perceived interests of the adoption establishment at the expense of adopted persons. They keep adopted persons in their place—retained in a secondary position, dependent on and subject to adoption industry practice and authority. "Critical to the whole idea of social discrimination is the fact that it is embedded in social structures and sustained by group practices" (Yinger, 1968, p. 449).

The non-adopted majority often fails to understand or appreciate what the denial of this basic right means to adopted persons. At one time, few in the majority identified differential treatment of blacks or women as discriminatory. Delete the word adoptee from proposed open record legislation—that includes provisions for contact and disclosure vetoes by birth and adoptive parents, for psychological counseling, for waiting periods, for an advanced age of majority—and substitute the word Jew, Black, Native American, Catholic, or woman. People might better understand why adopted persons object strongly.

Adoptive status carries with it social disgrace, disapproval, and legally sanctioned discrimination that denies adopted persons first-class citizenship. Only adopted persons are denied their genealogy by law. Likewise, only adoptees are issued a birth certificate that represents a legalized fraud. Arguments put forward to deny adult adopted citizens that which all other citizens have—direct access to their original birth record and the right to know their origins—are rationalizations in defense of discrimination.

References

Adoptees and balancing equities. (1978, November 22). *The Washington Star*, p. A.

Barringer, F. (1978). Adopted children urge change in law. *The Washington Post,* pp. A1, A12.

Bentzen, M. (1978, April 2). Roots (Letters to the Washington Post Magazine). *The Washington Post*, p. 63.

Crawford, V. (1979, March 6). *Testimony.* Presented at the Maryland Senate Judicial Proceedings Committee hearing on S. B. No. 837, Annapolis, MD.

Dressler, D. (1969). *Sociology: The study of human interaction.* New York: Alfred A. Knopf.

Folkenberg, J., Harrington, J., & Saba, J. (1979, March 6) *Adult adoptee's sealed birth records.* Paper presented at the Maryland Senate Judicial Proceedings Committee Hearing on S. B. No. 837, Annapolis, MD.

Goodman, E. (1979, February 20). A new look at adoption. *The Washington Post,* p. A15.

Haase, T. (1977, March 31). Adoptees push right to records. *The Montgomery Journal.*

Hardy, W. J. (1979, April, 24). Pinnacle of selfishness. *The Washington Post,* p. A19.

Hewit, M., & Pinchbeck, I. (1969). *Children in English society.* London: Kegan Paul, Trench, Trubner & Co.

Kadushin, A. (1974) *Child Welfare Se*rvices (2nd ed.). New York: Macmillan Publishing Company.

References

LeShan, E. J. (1974, May). *You and your adopted child. (No. 274).* [Brochure] New York, NY: Public Affairs Committee.

LeShan, E. J. (1977, March). Should adoptees search for their "real" parents? *Women's Day, 40,* 214, 218.

Means, M. (1978). Keep records closed on child adoption. New York*: King Features Syndicate.*

Small, J. W. (1977). *A comparison of genetic identity indicators between adopted and non-adopted adults.* Unpublished master's thesis, The Catholic University of America, Washington, DC.

Stein, J. (Ed.). (1967). *The Random House dictionary of the English language.* (Unabridged ed.). New York: Random House.

White, J. M. (1975, May 11). Adoptees: opening doors to the past or a Pandora's box? *The Washington Post, pp.* K1, K10.

Wilson, T. R. (1971, July 12). *The New York Daily News.*

Wright, C. (1978, February 26). Who am I? *The Washington Post Magazine.* pp. 9, 10, 12, 13, 15, 17.

Yinger, M. J. (1968). Prejudice: social discrimination. In D. L. Sills (Ed.), *International encyclopedia of social scie*nces (1st. ed.). London: Macmillan/The Free Press.

Anti-Adoptee Media Bias

A spate of anti-adoptee journalism surfaced recently, fueled by Measure 58—The Adoptee Rights Initiative—that Oregon voters passed by a 57 to 43 % margin in November, 1998. Measure 58 restores equal rights to adults born and adopted in Oregon. That means that they will have the same access to the uncensored government record of their birth as non-adopted Oregonians. The right to their original birth certificate was abrogated in 1957—a fact that some folks fail to realize, or prefer to overlook. In any event, the furor has publicly unmasked adoption's darker side. It has reached the level of adoptee bashing, and more.

Senior Washington Post political editor David Broder (2,000, May 21) opines that through ballot initiatives citizens voted to " . . . allow adopted children to obtain the names of their biological parents" (para. 3). That is not true. The fact is Measure 58 addresses the rights of adult adopted citizens. Yet many people do keep labeling these 30, 40, 50 and 60-year-old persons as adopted children. Actually, the media reflect a pertinacious pattern of adult adoptee infantilism.

Adoption Has a Positive Value, But . . .

Editorials and reports that enhance adoption's warm and fuzzy side are consonant with the positive value society places on adoption. Washington Post columnist Mary McGrory (2002, November 28) touts adoption and National Adoption Day. Under the headline, "Giving Thanks for The Gift of Family" McGrory writes:

> . . . From the start, you knew it was going to be a different sort of day at the District of Columbia Superior court . . . pastel balloons . . . stuffed toys . . . and 22 children were officially becoming part of 15 families . . . . Across the nation, more than 1,400 children began belonging to new parents (p. A 47).

Adult adopted person's experience and the status of adopted person's rights is dissonant with a warm and fuzzy perspective. Efforts on the part of adopted adults to assert the restoration of their rights makes some people uncomfortable, and even hostile. For them, the concepts of adoptees as adults and adoptee's rights are unfamiliar and threatening. Hence, reports that diminish adopted person's stature, defame adoptive status, or detract from the significance and importance of adoptee's civil rights are common.

Adoptee Bashing . . .

What many editorials and articles reveal is a prejudice that is widespread, unrestrained and entrenched. And does that affect truth, fact, and fairness in reporting? Yes. Though bigotry toward adopted persons is not exclusive to the press. They are just folks that happen to write for a living. It is their access to the public that allows for active dissemination and perpetuation of their bias. More injurious yet, the media mirrors the dominant views of legislators, a couple of prominent advice columnists, and John and Jane Q. Public. It is a point that recently retired journalist Judy Mann (2001, December 28) corroborates. In her farewell essay Mann says, "I have always felt that the media mirror society . . . " (p. C8).

So from whence comes adoptee bashing? Is there an object to defaming adopted persons? A dear friend believes he knows from whence the bigotry comes. He says, "It comes with our mother's milk." He is referring to sets of beliefs that are highly enduring, well ingrained in the dominant culture, and seldom questioned. They pass from parent to child, and are learned at an early age. Thus, folks come to believe that there is something wrong with adopted persons. They learn that the circumstance of an adopted person's birth is different, since most are born out of wedlock. Nearly everyone understands that labels like illegitimate and bastard convey adoptive status. They also connote cultural disapproval. Correspondingly, society considers adopted persons to be a product of bad seed. So they are damaged goods, or second best. These are the archetypes for adopted persons, the glue that connects adoption to shame and scandal. They are at the heart of the print media's adoptee bashing and their anti-adoptee slant toward Measure 58.

The Denver Rocky Mountain News

Under a Denver Rocky Mountain News (Gutierrez & Gonzales, 1999, December 12) headline "Teen Held In Family Killings: Longmont Boy Arrested in Slayings of His Adoptive Mother and Grandmother," references to the boy's adoptive status appear five more times in the story that follows:

> A 14-year old boy was held Saturday in the slayings of his adoptive mother and grandmother at their home in an affluent . . . neighborhood (para. 1).

> Neighbors and family members identified the boy as Engel's adopted son, John (para. 4).

> John Engel . . . was adopted more than 10 years ago . . . (para. 10).

> The couple also adopted a girl . . . (para. 12).

> Friends and neighbors lauded the parents for adopting the boy and girl (para. 16).

That appears to be a blatant attempt to assign causality. The press routinely cites adoptive status when a crime story is reported. Nonadoptive status is never implicated in like fashion.

The Oregonian

Readers learn from the March 25, 2000 headline of The Oregonian newspaper that "Killer of Adoptive Parents Hails Move." The subtitle "Patrick Niiranen Sees Himself Closer to Learning the Identity of His Biological Parents" tells them more. In the story that follows Associated Press reporter Charles E. Beggs writes:

> An inmate who beat his adoptive parents to death with a hammer in their Southeast Portland home said Friday he was delighted that a law that could help him find the identities of his birth parents might be close to taking effect . . . (para. 1).

> "I jumped for joy," said Patrick Niiranen, who said he has been on a lifelong quest to find his biological parents (para. 2).

Niiranen is referring to Oregon's Measure 58. In the third paragraph of the story readers learn that "The Oregon Supreme Court on Tuesday [March

21, 2000] refused to review a lower court ruling that upheld [Measure 58] the law, clearing the way for it to take effect April 12" (para. 3).

The Grant's Pass Daily Courier

In The Grant's Pass Daily Courier editorial "Flawed Law Puts Adoptee's Rights Before Parents," Dan Guthrie (1999, January 28) writes:

> People are having second thoughts about Measure 58 (para. 1).

> This trend setting law gives adult, Oregon-born adoptees . . . their birth certificates. Voters passed it . . . after a campaign by a band of militant adoptees . . . claimed they have a right to the identities of their birth parents. They were outraged at being denied . . . [their] heritage . . . (para. 2).

> Several birth mothers challenged [M 58] . . . arguing that it breached [the] confidentiality they were guaranteed when choosing to bear rather than abort infants. They were appalled at the prospect of estranged children showing up decades later on their doorsteps (para. 3).

Guthrie suggests possible legislative "improvements," like a registry:

> . . . that gives adoptees the names of their birth parents—but only with the parent's permission (para. 5).

> Such a registry would not satisfy the adoptees who feel their . . . rights are being violated. For them emotions run too high for compromise (para. 6).

This emotionalism has left many uneasy about [M 58]. The only factual argument offered by adoptees concerns their need for medical records . . . (para. 7).

A fairy tale cloud hovers over their rhetoric (para. 9).

There is also an element of disrespect for the adoptive parents in all this. The folks who stood by [the adoptees] in deed and need are being told [that] they don't completely fill the bill (para. 10).

Finally, Guthrie says sociologists estimate that:

. . . up to two of every 10 Oregon children are fathered by somebody other than the presumed biological dad . . . (para. 11).

We should have a national DNA databank so [everyone]—not just adoptees—can learn the true identities of [their] birth parents (para. 12).

Some secrets are better left alone (para. 13).

The San Francisco Examiner

Beneath the headline, "Fight Over Adoption Secrecy," The San Francisco Examiner (1999, February 22) editorializes that:

Oregon voters set off a 21-year time bomb. Explosions are already being heard (para. 2).

The Oregon measure is . . . on hold because a group of birth mothers has sued, arguing that state statues promise them confidentiality . . . (para. 5).

> In the meantime, lives—although not yet shattered—are crumbling, revealing the fault lines of heartbreak on which they've been built (para. 6).

> Anguish is everywhere in the adoption equation . . . . the birth mother . . . adoptive parents . . . . adopted children haunted by phantom birth parents who, they may feel "abandoned" them—beings . . . . they cannot know. Phantom limbs on the family tree (para. 10).

The Examiner refers to Helen Hill, the 43 year old mother, art therapist, sheep farmer and chief petitioner of Measure 58 as, " . . . an adoptee and member of Bastard Nation, a radical adoptee-rights group" (para. 12). The Examiner opines:

> It's almost as if the angry children of Bastard Nation who fought so hard for Measure 58 are outing their own mothers. Where is the concern for a mother confronted by an angry, perhaps dangerous child (para. 16)?

> Adoption laws are remnants of another era—when only "bad" girls got pregnant . . . . laws need to be humanely amended, but the initiative process and its simplistic reduction of a sensitive issue is not the way to go (para. 18).

Time Magazine

Time magazine captions a story about Measure 58, "Tracking Down Mom" (p. 64). A subordinate headline asks readers, "Should adopted children have the right to uncover their birth parents" (p. 64)? The article, written by John Cloud (1999, February 22) is juxtaposed to a shadowy female image, an apparent symbol of the quintessential shamed and hapless birthmother.

Cloud cautions that Measure 58:

> . . . will radically change traditional adoption law by allowing adoptees the unfettered right to see their birth certificate when they turn 21. . . . the law would mean adoptees . . . could easily find Mom's real name—and perhaps track her down (p. 64).

> Before the late '60's, states thought they were doing birth mothers a favor by confining their identities to dusty registrar's books. At the time, only "bad" girls got pregnant out of wedlock . . . (p. 64). Today, of course, that attitude, seems quaintly outmoded . . . . We have become sensitized to the rights of adoptees . . . (p. 65).

> Several states have [contrived] . . . workable new laws to help . . . without treading on the rights of mothers. It's a tricky legislative game. . . . birthmothers . . . saying they were promised . . . lifelong confidentiality . . . (p. 65).

> . . . the initiative process which encourages simplistic laws, like Oregon's Measure 58, has not provided a solution. It will take more careful legislation to let adoptees feel whole, even as [some birthmothers] of the nation feel safe (p. 65).

An Assault On Adoptee's Rights

The choice of headlines sensationalizes, misrepresents, distorts, and misinforms. Adopted persons are stereotyped and stigmatized. Look at the attempt to impugn and denigrate them. If that is not media manipulation in pursuit of an assault on adopted persons, and adopted person's rights, then what is?

Measure 58 is about restoring adoptee's rights to direct access to the uncensored record of their birth that the state of Oregon abrogated just 41 years ago. To set the record straight Measure 58 is not about children, not about parent's rights, and not about tracking down anyone's mom. Yet, that is what these journalists wrote about.

Questions

It all justifies asking, "Did the journalists do their homework? Did they check their sources? Did they apply principles of fairness and responsibility in their reports? Had they read *The Oregon Adoptee Rights Initiative 1998* brochure authored by The Oregon 'Open 98' Committee"?

Answers

Question (9) of *The Oregon Adoptee Rights Initiative 1998* brochure asks, "Will passage of this initiative violate the rights of a birth mother" (para. 9)? The answer is no. A 1997 decision by the U.S. Court of Appeals for the 6th Circuit Court (Doe v. Sundquist), ruled that no one has a constitutional right to preserve his or her anonymity from their offspring. The court opined:

> A birth is simultaneously an intimate occasion and a public event—the government has long kept records of when, where, and by whom babies are born. Such records have myriad purposes, such as furthering the interest of children in knowing the circumstances of their birth (question 9).

That decision was not reported in the editorials and article cited above.

Nowhere in the Examiner and the Daily Courier editorials or Time article was a reference made to a NY Times "Letter to the Editor," "Adoptees Have Rights" written by Madelyn Freundlich (1999, February 5), then Director of the Evan B. Donaldson Adoption Institute. She said:

> A Feb. 1 editorial [NY Times] assumes that measures like the one passed in Oregon that provide adult adoptees with access to their birth certificates break promises of confidentiality made to birth mothers . . . (para. 1).

> In fact, no document of surrender has ever been produced containing a promise of confidentiality, and given that adoption records in every state may be opened by courts upon showing of good cause, no such promise of confidentiality could legitimately be made (para. 2).

Now about the question, "Will adoption rates decrease if original birth records are opened to adopted adults"? The editorials and the Time article also omitted data regarding Alaska and Kansas, states in which adult adoptees may access their original birth records. Abortion rates there are lower than for the US as a whole. The National Center for Court Statistics reports that the 1992 rate of adoptions per thousand live births was 31.2 nationally. It was 53.5 in AK and 48.6 in KS *(The Oregon Adoptee Rights Initiative 1998,* question 14).

Defamation of adopted persons is not limited to adoptee activists or Measure 58. Anti-adoptee attitudes as evidenced in The Examiner, The Daily Courier, and Time magazine cast aspersions on all people that believe adoption is an acceptable, even a positive way to join a family. It is germane to adoptive parents that realize that once their child's adoptive status is revealed, other people's perceptions of their child may become permanently altered and negatively influenced. There are still some people for whom the label adoptee is but a euphemism for bastard.

The Washington Post

In a straightforward report to The Washington Post, headlined, "Oregon Court Upholds Law Giving Adoptees Access to Birth Records," Associated Press reporter Charles E. Beggs (1999, December 30) writes:

> The Oregon Court of Appeals today [December 29] upheld the nation's first voter-passed law to give adult adoptees access to their original birth certificates (para. 1).

> A three-judge panel unanimously held that birth mothers have no constitutional right to have the records kept confidential (para. 2).

> The court also lifted an injunction barring the state Health Division from releasing the Records (para. 3).

> . . . The National Council for Adoption, said the ruling opens the door to birth mothers being harassed by children they gave up for adoption years ago . . . understanding they would never be contacted (para. 8).

> "The state of Oregon is saying to all of the people who were promised privacy in the past, 'We were lying to you,' " said Bill Pierce, spokesman for the Washington, DC-based group [National Council for Adoption] (para. 9).

> Deputy Attorney general David Schuman had argued . . . that the "right to anonymous adoption was invented in

1957," referring to the [Oregon] Legislature's passage of a law that year sealing what had been open records (para. 13).

"At no time in Oregon's history have the adoption laws required the consent of, or even notice to, a birthmother on the opening of adoption records or sealed birth certificates," the appeals court said in an opinion written by Judge Paul De Muniz (para. 16).

Private Interests

So who benefits from adoptee bashing? The industry's highly lucrative private sector stands to benefit the most from anti-adoptee media bias. Actually, what these adoption attorneys, special interests groups, and private agencies do is actively lobby and litigate to maintain and defend a closed adoption system. Their role is self-serving and protective.

Some credit for the development of organized opposition to restoring adoptee's rights goes to The Model State Adoption Act (1978). It was the first comprehensive adoption law written under Federal sponsorship. Title V. Records, Section 502. Birth Certificates, subsection (d) would open the original birth certificate to adult adopted persons, upon a simple request: no court order or intervention would be required. Title V, subsection (d) posed a specific threat to the private adoption sector (Model State Adoption Act, 1978, pp. 213-214).

The Edna Gladney Home and other private adoption agencies coalesced and scuttled the Model Act. They formed The National Council for Adoption (NCFA), and hired professional anti-adoptee rights lobbyist William Pierce. Under the cloak of child welfare, Pierce set the current anti-adoptee rights theme. The distortions, fabrications, and misinformation that are NCFA propaganda are effective. The editorials and the Time magazine article are redolent with NCFA influence. And there is more to come.

The St. Petersburg Times

When the Oregon Supreme Court refused to review a lower court hearing upholding voter approved Measure 58, the media bit again. In this round, a St. Petersburg Times (January 9, 2000) headline declared, "Adoptees Confuse Curiosity With Rights." Huh? Robyn Blumner says:

> In case you haven't heard the noise, there's another group out there clamoring for "civil rights." It's adoptees. Some are so desperate to find their genetic connections, they are lobbying for laws to pry open sealed adoption records (para. 1).

> When [mothers] . . . gave up their children for adoption, they were assured confidentiality. Sadly, courts are refusing to give force to these promises . . . (para. 2).

> Don't get me wrong. There's no doubt heredity plays a large role . . . . I would argue our genes are far more important than environmental factors . . . . And while this interest is understandable, it simply doesn't rise to a civil or human right (para. 4).

> Somehow . . . adoptees have been successful in convincing legislators and the public that the satisfaction of their curiosity overrides any confidentiality promised the birth mothers (para 7).

> Wanting to know one's genetic links is an understandable desire, but adoptees already know who their

real parents are—the mom and dad who supported and nurtured them. The other set gave them up and moved on. So should they (para. 12).

Well, about adoptee's rights, Ms. Blumner?

The Chicago Tribune

Then in a Chicago Tribune editorial, January 13, 2000, "Taking Privacy Out of Adoption," Steve Chapman opines:

Somewhere in America today, there is a young, unmarried woman who has suddenly found herself pregnant (para. 1).

Given the Supreme Court's judgment that her constitutional right to privacy includes the right to get an abortion, she can terminate her pregnancy . . . . Or she can . . . endure the pregnancy, give birth, and put her baby up for adoption (para. 2).

If she chooses adoption, she can . . . keep her identity confidential . . . (para. 3).

But in Oregon, this . . . assurance is gone. Under [Measure 58] . . . upheld last month by a state appeals court, adoptees now have the right to obtain their original birth certificates . . . (para. 4).

It's not hard to understand and sympathize with . . . adopted children to find out who their biological parents were . . . (para. 7).

> But when a woman decides to give up a child, she ought to have the option of keeping her identity a secret . . . . It's the height of presumption to overrule her (para. 9).

> It would be nice [to] accommodate . . . people . . . adopted 20 or 30 years ago. But we shouldn't . . . at the expense of children not yet conceived whose mothers might . . . choose adoption. Twenty or 30 years from now, if the Oregon approach prevails, many . . . children won't be asking for . . . birth records . . . Many of them will have never been born (para. 13).

Ouch! So now Measure 58 is about maintaining supply and fulfilling demand?

About the Industry

Perhaps these journalists are confused. NCFA has cooked up a veritable stew of, um, facts. If the privacy and protection arguments are wearing thin, throw in abortion rates, and the kitchen sink, as well. Taking in NCFA's anti-adoptee rights propaganda is like accepting the facts about tobacco, addiction, and cancer from tobacco industry lobbyists.

The NCFA lobbies for passage of the Uniform Adoption Act (UAA). The UAA would seal adoption records for 99 years, and criminalize searching. Drafted by the National Conference of Commissioners on Uniform State Laws (NCCUSL), support comes from the private sector of the adoption industry, and other agencies, attorneys, and adoption professionals that believe adoptee's rights legislation is a threat to their livelihood. The NCFA is joined by Latter Day Saints-affiliated adoption agencies, Pat Robertson's American Center for Law and Justice (ACLJ), the

Christian Coalition, The Family Research Council and other "defenders of the status quo" (Babb, 1997, retrieved 2003, January 24 from http://www.bastards.org/activism/babb.htm).

Make no mistake about it, NCFA's message—that information about an adopted person's birth, origins and relinquishment is so shameful it must be locked away for all time—is a means to an end, and NCFA intends to protect their share of the industry. Pierce's pitch, "What about protection of the birthmother?" and "Birth mothers were promised confidentiality," excludes the fact that adopted persons are denied equal protection, due process and equal access to information. And sealing of adoptee's birth records perpetuates discrimination as it maintains and protects secrets and lies. Pierce is to adopted person's civil rights as David Duke is to black civil rights.

Caught unawares by the passage of Measure 58, NCFA underestimated the rapidity with which the grass roots adoptee civil rights movement has caught fire. It is over the restoration of their civil rights that adopted persons have found their voice. When the Oregon Adoptee Rights Initiative 1998 presented voters with a clear, narrow, and focused issue—equal protection and due process for all of Oregon's citizens, the voters got the message, and responded with fairness and equality.

Adopted persons are set apart by the circumstances of their birth, and subsequent family status. The abrogation of adopted person's civil rights is based solely on their adoptive status, a reason that is wholly beyond their control. Society professes to value adoption, but practices adoptee intolerance. Negative adoptee archetypes are embedded in the cultural psyche. The resultant discrimination is based on a deep mistrust of adopted persons as a class. What makes past NCFA director Bill Pierce's anti-adoptee rights rhetoric work like a hot knife through butter? He simply reinforces negative adoptee archetypes. He taps the minds of John and Jane Q Public, those legislators, and the media, for whom adoptees as a class are mistrusted—their motives, maturity and mental status automatically suspect—and their anti-sociality presumed.

References

Babb, L. A. (1997). *Defenders of the status quo*. Abstracted January 20, 2003, from http://www.bastards.org/activism/babb.htm

Beggs, C. E. (1999, December 30). Oregon court upholds law giving adoptees access to birth records. *The Washington Post*, p. A08.

Beggs, C. E. (2,000, March 25). Killer of adoptive parents hails move. *The Oregonian.*

Blumner, R. E. (2000, January 9). Adoptees confuse curiosity with rights. *St. Petersburg Times*, p. 3 D.

Broder, D. S. (2,000, May 21). The ballot initiative: Fed up with government, voters now seek to pass laws themselves. *The Washington Post.*

Chapman, S. (2,000, January 13). Taking the privacy out of adoption. *The Chicago Tribune*, p. 23.

Cloud, J. (1999, February 22). Tracking down Mom. *Time*, pp. 64-65.

Fight over adoption secrecy. (1999, February 22). *The San Francisco Examiner.*

Freundlich, M. (1999, February 5). [Letter To the Editor]. *The New York Times.*

Guthrie, D. (1999, January 28). Flawed law puts adoptee's rights before parents. *The Grant's Pass Daily Courier.*

Gutierrez, H., & Gonzales, M. (1999, December 12). Teen held in family killings: Longmont boy arrested in slayings of his adoptive mother and grandmother. *The Denver Rocky Mountain News.*

Mann, J. (2001, December 28). A farewell wish: That women will be heard. *The Washington Post,* p. C8.

References

McGrory, M. (2002, November 28). Giving thanks for the gift of family. *The Washington Post,* p. A47.

Model State Adoption Act. (1979, October). U. S. Department of Health, Education, and Welfare. Office of Human Development Services Administration for Children, Youth, and Families, Children's Bureau.

The Oregon adoptee rights initiative 1998. (1998). Nehalem, Oregon: The Open 98 Committee.

About Open Records

Open record bills continue to spring up in state legislatures around the country. In some states there are even multiple bills backed by competing interests. Then there is the evil Uniform Adoption Act (UAA) drafted by the National Conference of Commissioners on Uniform State Laws (NCCUSL). The UAA would seal birth and adoption records for 99 years and criminalize searching. Support for the UAA comes primarily from those agencies and professionals that perceive restoration of adopted person's civil rights a threat to their livelihood. All this legislative activity is generating discussion, differentiation, discovery, and debate. What is different this legislative go around is that folks are paying closer attention to what each bill provides and which groups focus on what interests. Now people are asking, "Open records"? "Which records"? "Who gets what"? "What restrictions apply"? "Is the focus on searches and reunions, or on restoring adopted persons civil rights"? Some have even begun to question whether the term open records might be a misnomer.

Perhaps that's because few if any of these open record bills serve the best interests of adopted persons, their offspring, and succeeding generations. To the contrary, most are primarily anti adoptee's rights. Let us explore the issues and look at the facts.

A Wrong Turn

At some point, folks advocating for open record legislation took a wrong turn. Consequently, the current crop of open record bills has little if anything to do with restoring and protecting adopted person's civil rights.

The current crop of open record bills is all about search and reunion. This direction is worthy of reconsideration.

Adopted Person's Civil Rights.

In the early 1970's adoptee activist and author, Florence Fisher (*The Search for Anna Fisher*, 1973) launched the adoptee civil rights movement. She founded The Adoptee Liberty Movement Association (ALMA). A proliferation of search and support groups followed. Some groups, like Adoptees In Search (AIS) advocated restoration of adopted person's civil rights and promoted open record legislation to unseal adopted person's birth records. Other groups focused more on reuniting adopted persons and their birth parents.

Adopted person's civil rights invariably become subordinated in those groups and organizations that combine the disparate goals of adopted persons, birth parents, and adoptive parents. Repeat: adopted person's civil rights invariably become subordinated in those groups and organizations that combine the disparate goals of adopted persons, birth parents, and adoptive parents.

The Model State Adoption Act

The 1978 Model State Adoption Act was the first comprehensive adoption law written under Federal sponsorship. The preamble states that "The adoption process shall treat all persons fairly, but the principle that adoption is a service for adoptees shall govern where rights are in conflict and compromise is not possible."

Title V of the Act deals with adoption records and addresses the retention of records, birth certificates, agency and court records, the treatment of records, retroactivity, etc. Subsection (d) provides that the original birth certificate will be opened to the adoptee that has attained majority upon the adoptee's simple request: no court order or intervention is required.

The Opposition

Alarmed by Title V of the Act, The Edna Gladney Home and other private adoption agencies banded together to scuttle the Model State Adoption Act. They formed the National Council for Adoption (NCFA). NCFA hired professional anti-adoptee rights lobbyist William Pierce to represent them. Pierce's pitches, "What about protection of the birth mother"? and "Birth mothers were promised confidentiality"! excludes the fact that it is adopted persons—not birth parents—that had their rights abrogated through adoption. Pierce and the NCFA work to deny to adopted persons the same rights and privileges that Pierce and other nonadopted persons value for themselves. Moreover, child welfare has long deemed adoption an institution traditionally and philosophically designed to serve children. This principle appears to be in jeopardy, maybe even passé, as evidenced by the current crop of open record bills.

The good news is that Pierce and his ilk are fighting a losing battle. The birthmother's need for protection and a right to privacy—from her own child—has been challenged, and denied. For more information on this case see Doe v. Sundquist on the American Adoption Congress (AAC) web site at (http://www.americanadoptioncongress.org) and click on "Courts Grant 'Supreme' Victory in Tennessee." The bad news is that open record legislation in Tennessee was all about search and reunions—never about the restoration of adopted person's civil rights. What passed as open record legislation there includes contact and disclosure vetoes, and criminal penalties for restriction violations.

Compromise or Capitulation?

Now some folks are merely paying lip service to the restoration of adopted person's civil rights. Many are actively supporting bills that include "contact" and "disclosure" vetoes. They are the stuff of search and reunion legislation. When a birthparent files a disclosure veto, they exercise a special right that permanently blocks their offspring's access to information pertaining to that person's lineage. A birth parent that files a contact veto prohibits their adult child, under criminal penalty, from making contact with them. Some folks euphemistically and derogatorily call these "compromise" bills. Others call it conditional access legislation. Perhaps it is more appropriate to call them "capitulation" bills. Compromise or capitulation bills virtually bury civil right issues for adopted persons.

Many supporters of search and reunion legislation believe that without compromise no open record bills will pass state legislatures. They argue that getting one state open is better than no state open. That sounds negative and defeatist. Besides, Kansas, Alaska, Alabama and Oregon are open record states. Moreover, the history of civil rights legislation amply demonstrates that it is difficult to overcome bad legislation, once it is in place. Think of Plessy v. Ferguson (1892) that allowed separate but equal classrooms for blacks and whites, and Brown v. the board of education that finally overturned it in 1954.

Some that support search and reunion legislation are actively involved in providing mandated confidential intermediary search services. It has become a small industry in itself. Its providers seem especially unable or unwilling to see how outrageous, self serving, objectionable, and discriminatory third party intervention is when mandated by open record legislation. Making a confidential intermediary system obligatory, not optional, is discrimination in its purest form.

Underlying the mandatory confidential intermediary system is an ugly and entrenched mistrust of adopted persons. Widespread prejudice flourishes under the guise of the need for confidentiality and protection of the parties to an adoption. That there is something wrong with adopted persons. That they are different. They are damaged goods. They come from bad seed. It is time to expose the prejudice and confront the discrimination these stereotypes foster.

A Right Turn

Look at what the folks at Bastard Nation (BN) have to say. Contact them at (http://www.bastards.org). BN is a grass roots organization dedicated to passage of legislation restoring adopted person's civil rights. It is because of their unambiguous stance that BN commands respect and support from pro adoptee rights advocates that include adopted persons, and adoptive and birth parents from across the country, and abroad.

Resolution

Adopted persons deserve equal rights with non-adopted persons. To achieve an equitable balance between adopted and non-adopted citizens, legislation is required to restore adopted person's rights to direct access to their birth records, at majority. Nothing more, nothing less.

Open Records Maryland Style 1997

Open record bills are springing up in state legislatures around the country. This development is creating excitement in many quarters. It is generating interest, debate, and passion. Still, some view what is happening with alarm and concern. In fact they find it chilling, and are urging caution. Why? Few, if any, of these open record bills appear to be in the best interests of adopted persons and their offspring.

There are conflicting views as to what the issues are, and how they might be resolved. There certainly are conflicting interests. How different folks feel about the facts differs greatly. Yet certain facts remain.

The basis for this report came from experience with open record bills introduced in the 1997 Maryland legislative session. The struggle over open records that took place there is similar to what is happening elsewhere, both in Canada and in the U. S.

We'll take a critical look at some of the provisions that appear in these open record bills, like disclosure vetoes, contact vetoes, and mandatory intermediaries; explore the essential differences between search and reunion and civil rights legislation; make suggestions and recommendations for evaluating open record legislation; and share some lessons learned.

A Certain Fact

Adopted persons are the only members of the triad—adoptees, adoptive parents and birth parents—that have lost their 14th Amendment right to equal protection and their First Amendment right to equal access to vital information through adoption. Folks adopted in Maryland lost their right to direct access to the original record of their birth in 1947.

Enactment of legislation to seal adopted person's birth records was based on recommendations from adoption workers, and was in accordance with standards set by the Child Welfare League of America (CWLA) in 1938. To date research shows no participation by adopted persons in the establishment of sealed record legislation. The procedure of sealing birth records fails to recognize that the adopted child becomes an adult at the age of majority.

The civil rights of adopted persons were abrogated for reasons that were and are beyond their control. They are singled out based solely on the nature of their family status as adopted persons. The state of Maryland withholds from them and their offspring basic identifying information about their social, ethnic and genetic heritage, including their familial health history. Except for adoption, there would be no abrogation of their rights, and no basis for prejudicial and discriminatory treatment.

Adopted persons are different. Their difference is what makes them suspect. It is through adoption that they become members of a suspect, second class of citizens.

Adopted persons must regain equal footing with non-adopted persons. That means direct access to their original birth record—nothing more and nothing less. Legislation that unseals the record of their birth, at their majority, will restore what was theirs 50 years ago. That is what is needed to achieve equality between Maryland's adopted and non-adopted citizens.

Would the open record legislation just defeated in Maryland have restored and protected adopted person's civil rights? Most certainly not!

"Dirty Little Secret" Legislation

The current crop of open record bills is shame based and discriminatory. Under the guise of confidentiality and protection lies an entrenched and widespread prejudice that few acknowledge or address. Essential to any shame based adoption legislation is the perception that adopted persons are dirty little secrets that come from bad seed. Shame based legislation serves to protect the status quo, as it maintains negative adoption stereotypes.

The current crop of open record bills—"dirty little secret" legislation— functions to deny, restrict, block, and isolate adopted persons from access to their heritage. It is not about restoring abrogated rights and privileges. Still, some consider these bills progressive. They are regressive. Institutions customarily hide their dirty laundry behind privacy rules. The adoption industry shields itself from accountability by keeping secrets and telling lies. These open record bills serve to protect and maintain a closed adoption system.

The Fight to Defeat Bad Legislation

A January 22, 1997 Baltimore Sun article "Rights Clash Over Adoption Bill" reported that Maryland legislative delegate Frank Turner, an adoptee, was sponsoring a bill with 59 other legislators, " . . . to open all the birth records of adoptees 25 years or older—unless either of their birth parents files forms specifically blocking that access." The Sun is referring to the disclosure veto and the contact veto. The Sun said, "The proposal thrills adoptees . . . "

Adoptees In Search (AIS)—one of the country's oldest and largest adopted persons search and support organizations—had struggled since the mid-1970's to achieve adoption law reform and restore adopted person's civil rights in Maryland and DC.

AIS members contacted the Baltimore Sun's ombudsman to protest the article's flip tone, wrote letters to the editors and faxed them copies of AIS's 8 page legislative position paper Adoption Reform: Competing Interests, and informed the Sun that AIS was adamantly opposed to passage of this legislation.

This year marked the first time, though for different reasons, that AIS, Catholic Charities, and The Barker Foundation, a private adoption agency, were united in opposition to open record legislation. Bastard Nation (BN) (http://www.bastards.org) joined the battle.

Maryland's 1997 open record bill passed the House but failed to get a favorable report out of the Senate Judiciary Committee, and was defeated.

Disclosure Vetoes and Contact Vetoes

The disclosure and contact vetoes contained in Maryland's 1997 open record legislation are there to "protect" birthparents from their "shame." Implicit in these provisions is the presumption that women that gave birth out of wedlock and relinquished their child to adoption need protection from their shame. A Maryland legislator that favored disclosure and contact vetoes told AIS, "You don't want some 'kid' showing up 40 years later, knocking on your door, and saying, 'Hi, Dad' "! A birthfather member of AIS scoffed "Would it be all right if the `kid' were President of the United States"?

The intent of disclosure vetoes is to maintain birth parent anonymity forever. They extend protection to include even the child that the parent bore and relinquished to adoption. But birth and adoption is hardly a secret to the birthmother or to the adopted person. It is to them that these events happened.

A disclosure veto gives birth parents an all-inclusive right to deny to their child access to the original record of their child's birth, barring their offspring from vital information about their genetic heritage. The state records a person's birth to insure them equality, individuality, and protection as provided under the Constitution. The disclosure veto grants birthparents the right to keep adopted people perpetually anonymous—even to themselves. Imagine blocking other Maryland citizens from doing their genealogy because a relative has a right to file a disclosure veto.

A contact veto allows a birthparent to file a statement that they do not wish contact with the person they put up for adoption, and prohibit that person from contacting them and sometimes any member of the birthparent's immediate family. Violation of a contact veto is often a criminal penalty that may be punishable by a fine, imprisonment, or both.

Search and Reunion vs. Civil Rights Legislation

Open record legislation before the 1997 Maryland legislature was all about searches and reunions and not about the restoration of adopted person's civil rights. Search and reunion legislation is different from and fundamentally incompatible with adoptee civil rights legislation. It has nothing whatsoever to do with placing adopted citizens on equal footing with non-adopted citizens. Indeed those that support search and reunion legislation bury the civil rights issue for adoptees. The passage of search and reunion legislation helps to nail the lid and seal the coffin on adopted person's attempts to restore their civil right to equal protection under the 14th Amendment, and equal access to information under the First Amendment.

Lawmakers that support search and reunion legislation seem to be working under the assumption that searching birthparents and adoptees have identical goals. They do not. Birthparents search for the child they relinquished to adoption. They have their own pedigree. By contrast, adopted persons do not search for "mommy and daddy." The majority of adopted persons say their mother and father are the parents that raised them. For them, the central point of a search is the need to know their identity—to find their roots. Nonetheless, legislators continue to misinterpret adopted persons search for information as an attempt to find another set of parents.

Search and reunion legislation decrees that all of the parties to the adoption are equal. They are not. The fact that adopted persons are not entitled to the same rights as non-adopted persons, including their birth and adoptive parents, is often minimized, trivialized and ignored.

The adoption industry, by decreeing that all parties to the adoption triad are equal, purports to achieve a balance between the rights of all the parties. What a crock! Consider that as adoption industry trade-speak. Institutions use it when they want to resist change and maintain the status quo.

An opinion rendered on January 31, 1979, by Judge June Green of DC Superior Court reads, "The court . . . is impelled to find that the privacy interests of the birth parents must bow to the interests of the adoptee and that any conflict between the interests of birth and adoptive parents and an adoptive child must be resolved in favor of the promotion of protection of the welfare of the child."

Think of search and reunion legislation as poison apples for adopted persons. It can look so good, but may be so bad. Some adopted persons may incorrectly assume that the worst case scenario cannot or will not happen to them. That no confidential intermediary is going to report that his or her birth relative filed a disclosure or contact veto. They may choose to bite the apple. But if a disclosure or contact veto has been filed, then what? Those folks may find the poison apple is lethal. They will have paid their money and submitted to a process that leaves them empty-handed and in criminal jeopardy. A contact or disclosure veto filed is contact or disclosure denied.

Mandatory Intermediaries

Maryland's open record legislation 1997 provided for an elaborate mandatory, confidential, intermediary system referred to as "Adoption Contact Services." It was budgeted at a half million dollars. A mandatory intermediary system is about the adoption industry maintaining power, control, and the status quo. It primarily serves the adoption industry, including adoption agencies, adoption attorneys, and the state's health and human services administration by promoting post adoption search and reunion services that require confidential intermediaries, investigators, bureaucrats, administrators, supervisors, support staff, and others.

Many in favor of the Maryland open record legislation 1997 seem not to recognize that adopted children become adopted adults at the age of majority. Adopted persons are teaching in Maryland's classrooms, performing open-heart surgery in Maryland's hospitals, managing Maryland's banks, and litigating in Maryland's courts. Still, the state says that adopted persons must not be allowed to manage their familial relationships without an intermediary. A mandatory intermediary system is bad social work because it is inherently paternalistic, unnecessarily intrusive, infantilizing, and dis-empowering.

Lessons Learned

- Some that jumped on the open record bandwagon in 1997 had not read Maryland's open record bills. The same was true for some delegates that sponsored the bill. They were unaware that these bills carried a criminal penalty of 90 days in jail and a $500.00 fine for searchers that failed to respect the restrictions of the bill. Most were aghast when those provisions were brought to their attention.

- People need to know exactly what the term open record means. What record is open, who gets it, what is included, and what restrictions apply? Will adopted adults have unrestricted access to their original birth certificate? Will a special age of majority, like age 25, 30, or 35 be legislated for adopted persons? Maryland open record legislation 1997 raised the age of majority for adopted persons to 25 years. Does the legislation apply only to those persons born and adopted before the date the bill goes into effect? Will it apply only to those persons born and adopted after the bill takes effect?

- It is important to keep watch over progress of the bills. Read copies of all of the amendments. Amendments can dramatically change the original bill and garner either newly formed support, or opposition. AIS's opposition to Maryland's open record legislation 1997 did not change, though the original legislation was gutted and rewritten, with changes proposed by AIS members. The criminal penalty came out. The age of majority for adopted citizens reverted from age 25 to 21 years. The disclosure veto and contact veto remained. An elaborate and costly mandatory confidential intermediary system was added to facilitate enforcement of the disclosure and contact vetoes.

- There is a massive need for public education. Most states have had adoption legislation on the books since the mid 1800's. The purpose of this legislation was to provide for a written record of the adoption of a child. States did not begin to seal birth and adoption records until the late 1930's-1940's. Kansas never sealed its records. Alaska has open records. Most persons born and adopted in Maryland before 1947 can get their records. In states like Ohio and Pennsylvania, adopted persons could get original birth certificates until fairly recently. Most folks do not know that the concept of adopted persons having access to their original birth record is neither new nor original.

Scotland's adoption laws have provided adult adopted persons access to their original birth record since 1930. A study of that provision, *In Search of Origins* (Triseliotis, 1973) led the British Parliament to apply it throughout Great Britain as the Children's Act of 1975. Finland and Israel allow adopted persons access to records. The United Nations Convention on the Rights of the Child, November 20, 1989 adopted articles II, VII, VIII, and IX that guarantee all children their birth heritage—even if adopted. Only countries such as Armenia, Bosnia, Botswana, Iraq, Libya, Saudi Arabia, Singapore, and the U.S. failed to ratify the treaty.

It is not a good idea to compromise when civil rights are at stake. A history of civil rights legislation demonstrates that bad legislation, once in place, is difficult to overcome.

Closing Thoughts

Dominant institutions always want to resist change, and to maintain power and control. Protection is the usual argument used by those that fear change. Folks apply it to protect neighborhoods and property values, social status and clubs, schools, jobs, and businesses. The adoption industry uses protection of birth parents and confidentiality of birth records to do the same.

The restrictive provisions in dirty little secret legislation, like those embedded in MD HB 214 and SB 114 Adoption Search, Contact, and Reunion Services and Access to Birth and Adoption Records, that passed the Maryland legislature in 1998, include mandatory confidential intermediaries, disclosure and contact vetoes, and intrusive, pre-search questionnaires. All bear comparison to poll taxes and literacy tests. They are obstacles designed to block a group of citizens from exercising equal rights.

Examples taken from the Mutual Consent Voluntary Adoption Registry and/or Adoption Search, Contact and Reunion Services, Confidential Intermediary Program Services, State of Maryland Department of Human Resources in their 25 item Adoptee-Pre-search Interview Questionnaire include:

(1.) What is your reason (motivation) for conducting this search and why have you chosen to initiate it at this time?

(13.) Are your adoptive parents aware of your desire to initiate a search? Are they supportive of your efforts?

(16.) Briefly describe your childhood and growing up years. Are there any current unresolved problems with your adoptive family?

(18.) Have you ever received counseling, treatment, medication, and hospitalization for any emotional, mental, chemical or substance abuse problems?

(19.) Briefly describe your personality. Are there currently any unresolved problems in your personal life like (drugs, alcohol, etc)?

(24.) How do you feel about the State's requirement for an interview to assess and discuss your readiness to proceed with the search process?

What is now required is legislation that restores the rights of all adopted persons to direct access to a copy of their original birth record. The fact that adopted person's rights were abrogated is usually overlooked. Those rights are theirs to reclaim.

Suggested Reading

Anderson, R. (1993). *Second choice: Growing up adopted.* Chesterfield, MO: Badger Hill Press.
A psychiatrist and adopted person analyzes adoption from his personal and professional perspectives.

Bartholet, E. (1993). *Family bonds. Adoption & the politics of parenting.* New York, Houghton Mifflin.
A Harvard Law professor and adoptive parent raises questions about the way society treats infertility, and shapes adoption.

Fisher, F. (1974). *The search for Anna Fisher.* New York: Fawcett.
An adopted person outlines her pioneering effort to search.

Hartman, A. (1984). *Working with adoptive families beyond placement.* New York: Child Welfare League of America.
A professor and dean emerita of Smith College School of Social Work writes a post-placement model for practitioners.

Kirk, H. D. (1985). *Adoptive kinship. A modern institution in need of reform.* Port Angeles, WA. Brentwood Bay, British Columbia: Ben-Simon Publications.
A sociologist, researcher, and adoptive parent examines the social and psychological meanings of adoption.

Kornheiser, T. (1983). *The baby chase.* New York: Macmillan Publishing Company.
A Washington Post sports columnist and an adoptive parent writes about the struggle he and his wife have with infertility, and their personal encounters with the adoption industry.

Krementz, J. (1982). *How it feels to be adopted.* New York: Alfred A. Knopf.
A photographic journal about adoption.

Lifton, B. J. (1988). *Lost and found: The adoption experience.* New York: Harper Collins.
An author, researcher, and adopted person writes about what it means to be adopted.

Loux, A. K. (1997). *The limits of hope. An adoptive mother's story.* Charlottesville, VA: University Press of Virginia.
A St. Mary's College professor of English and an adoptive parent breaks the unwritten code of silence regarding the adoption of hard to place children.

Pertman, A. (2000). *Adoption nation. How the adoption revolution is transforming America.* New York: Basic Books.
An award winning journalist and adoptive parent explores some of the changes in adoption that affect current practice.

Saffian, S. (1998). *Ithaka. A daughter's memoir of being found.* New York: Basic Books.
An author and adopted person writes about self-discovery, the adoption experience, and the meaning of family.

Sorosky, A. D., Baran, A., and Pannor, R. (1989). *The adoption triangle.* San Antonio, TX: Corona.
A psychiatrist and two social workers research adopted persons, adoptive and birthparents and take exception to traditional adoption practice.

Strauss, J. A. S. (1994). *Birthright: The guide to search and reunion for adoptees, birth parents, and adoptive parents.* New York: Penguin.
An author and adopted person writes about the practical and emotional concerns that surround a search.

Subject Index

Abuse-excuse defense, 11
Adopted child pathology, 11,
29, 37, 98
Adopted child syndrome
  (ACS), 11, 30, 37
Adopted children
adjustment of, 19, 33, 34, 41
adjustment to adoption, 19
adolescence, 49-53
affectionless character, 40-41
age at time of placement, 41
analytic literature on, 37, 51
attitudes toward, 58
clean break legislation, 55
consigned to childhood, 18
deficit perspective, 9-11
disturbances in early object
  relations, 37, 65
genealogical bewilderment,
10, 29, 33, 38, 49, 65, 98
grow up, viii, xiv, 77, 82, 119
identity formation, 37,
49, 50, 51
in psychiatric service, 34, 79
intra-psychic life of, 98, 99
labeling of, 29, 125, 127
lost child, 78
maladjustment, 34, 37, 53
narcissistic injury to, 33, 37,
90
oedipal issues, 37, 42
out of wedlock birth, 58, 70,
110, 111
overrepresentation of, 34
perceptions of, 30, 37, 135
prolongation of family
  romance, 37, 46, 48-49,

65, 98
psychiatric problems, vii, xiv, 34
psychoanalytic theory and, 37,
44, 51, 54, 55
psychopathology of, 11, 29,
30, 35, 37, 55, 65, 98
scapegoat, 78-80, 104
symptom bearers, 104
units of treatment, 65, 83, 104
Adopted persons
abrogation of rights, xiii, xv, 5,
120, 124, 133, 147, 154, 155, 164
"Bad Adoptee," 79
bad seed, 2, 9, 57, 70, 98, 118,
127, 149, 155
bastard(y), 2, 57, 98, 127, 135
being adopted, xiii, 2, 29, 31,
34, 36, 58, 69, 72, 75, 80, 81,
98, 103
being different, 68, 89, 90, 92, 118
bigotry toward, 126, 127
birth and adoption records, 5, 8,
31, 55, 66, 67, 99, 109, 110, 117,
145, 161
civil rights, xv, 119, 126, 137, 140,
145, 146, 148, 149, 153-156, 158
closeted, xvii, 23, 111
damaged goods, 57, 127, 149
dirty little secrets, 155
discrimination against, xv, 109,
111, 117, 118, 121, 140, 141, 149
equal protection, 140, 154, 158
equal rights, 125, 150, 163
estimates of, 6, 97, 117
genetic ego, 52
genetic identity, xiv, 52, 69,
77, 102

shame, 1-3, 5, 12, 17, 23, 56,
71, 73-75, 88, 91, 93, 104,
118, 127, 131, 140, 155, 157
social convention, 1, 30
substitute for, 1, 3, 30, 31, 38,
50, 52, 109
taboo, vii, xvii, 2
viable alternate, 12
Adoption industry
accountability, 155
balance of rights, 159
bestows special rights, 120
emergence of, 7
fundamental adoption myth,
14, 31
image, vii, xviii, xix
lobbyists, xiii, 136, 139
maintenance of status quo,
xv, 140, 155, 159, 160
power and control, vii, 160,
162
practice and authority, 120
private sector, 136, 139
propaganda, xviii, 137, 139
protect shares, 140
protection, confidentiality,
140, 162
reforms, vii
worker's threatened, 119
Adoption Insights, xvii
Adoption Mystique, xix
Adoption policy and practice
ancestral connections, 50
artificiality factor, 13, 30
attitudes, vii, xix, 3, 8, 99,100
clean break, 8, 50, 67, 98, 99
closed, 3, 5, 16, 20, 82, 98
culture, 57
denial, 13, 14, 67, 82
expectations, 4, 5, 30, 31, 65,
70, 72, 87, 99, 100
family theory, xiv, 99

influences on, 3, 7, 8, 10, 98,
105, 106
paternalism, 3, 23, 82, 160
protection, 4, 5, 9, 15, 16, 31, 67,
82, 98, 100, 105, 109, 117-120,
140, 149, 154, 155, 162
repression, 23
sealing records, 5, 6, 8, 9, 13, 14,
18, 31, 55, 66, 67, 72, 82, 99,
109, 110, 145, 150, 154
secrecy, 4, 5, 66, 67, 72, 82, 101,
140, 154
shame based, 1, 3, 5, 23, 155
suppression, 23
telling, 87
traditional adoption practice, 65,
70, 72, 99, 100, 105
Adoption Search, Contact, and
Reunion Services, 163
Adoptive family
as variant, vii, 4, 81
co-dependence, 69, 70, 73, 78, 82
differences, 10, 12-14, 20, 30, 68,
72, 73, 81, 82, 90, 93, 98-103
dysfunction, 65, 67, 82, 103, 104
feelings, vii, xvii, 21, 65, 70-72,
87, 88, 100, 103, 104
influence, 4, 66
kinship, 6, 14, 30, 42, 97
loss, 20, 33, 68, 69, 89, 102
members, 3, 5, 6, 23, 65, 68, 70,
82, 87, 97, 99, 100-103, 106
minority status, 12, 33, 67, 90, 99
parent-child bond, 12, 67, 101
psychological child, 101
psychological parent, 101
scapegoat, 78, 79, 80, 104
secrets, 75, 82, 91, 100
social milieu, 12, 88
structure, 4, 10, 12, 20, 57, 68, 99,
104
truth, 105

Author Index

Afterword

I began to sense in my early thirties that there was something puzzling about adoption -- something outside my experiences with it -- more about how others viewed it -- though putting a name to what that is came much, much later.

I made a stab at it in 1979 when I wrote "The Dark Side of Adoption." It was testimony before a panel that included child welfare professionals heading state and county welfare departments and public and private agencies, policy makers, attorneys, a pediatrician, a juvenile court judge, and a NJ state legislator. They really needed to hear the adoptive person's perspective. I used words like prejudice, stigma and discrimination, but I did not yet perceive the extent of the problem, nor could I put a name to it.

Publishers encourage, even require authors to describe their book in a sentence or two. As I wrote my book I learned that telling people it was about adoption did not work. Mention adoption and people almost invariably associate it with a process, or reveal that a friend or relative adopted. To me, adoption means a way of living that encompasses a lifetime. It is how I identify myself and how others identify me.

I came to realize that adoption means something different to adopted persons than it does to adoptive parents or birthparents, though we use the word interchangeably. I believe this has led to problems when communicating about adoption. Understanding and accepting that giving up a child, adopting, or being adopted are entirely separate experiences associated with different, conflicting, and even competing perspectives may help.

I kept at it. I said, "My book is about adoption's aftermath…about what happens after an adoption." Too often, I heard, "Oh!" and I sensed that I was still off the mark.

Finally, I began to research social stigma in the summer of 2003 for an essay subsequently titled "Adoption: A Study in Stigma." The pieces started to fall into place. I Googled "differentness" and found a reference, credited to an adoptive parent who had been adopted herself. She writes about her painful loss of "normal" status, attributed to a difference of a "less desirable kind," because of the stigma "born by adoption." (Benward, Retrieved July 30, 2003 from www.pactadopt.org/press/articles/differentness.html).

In *Stigma: Notes on the Management of Spoiled Identity,*" Erving Goffman (1963, p. 3) describes stigma as "an attribute that is deeply discrediting."

Stigma represents socially constructed, negatively valued differences. Stigma, associated with shame, disgrace, dishonor and humiliation, is central to adoption. I realized for the first time that negative social stigma is the common denominator for every essay in my book

It underlies failed child welfare policies and practices that impede reform. It permeates the psychoanalytic literature on the adopted child, psychopathologizing adopted persons, in particular, and adoptive parents, birthmothers, and infertility. It inspires widespread anti-adoptee media bias. It results in discrimination and a loss of equal rights for adopted persons. It causes problems with how, when, what or whether to tell a child he or she was adopted, and what, when whether or how much parents should tell teachers, neighbors, family and friends. A system of non-constructive and dysfunctional myths maintains and supports the stigma.

Arguably, its clearest, most public manifestation is in the oppressive, repressive, unequal treatment of adopted persons as non-entities, their heritage held hostage by the District of Columbia and forty-five out of fifty states.

I was finally able to describe *The Adoption Mystique* as being a hard-hitting exposé about the powerful negative social stigma that permeates child adoption in the United States. My book falls under the genre of what I call adoption vérité.

Some folks say, "What stigma? I didn't know there was any stigma in adoption." I suggest that is akin to saying to an African American, "What racism? I didn't know there was any racism in America."

Others make an immediate connection. "Sure, I'd say there is stigma in adoption. We have a niece who is adopted. But my husband wouldn't consider it. He says that when these kids get to be teenagers, they could come and murder us in our beds."

A friend served on the board of a national search and support organization. She conducted monthly search workshops, wrote letters to editors, gave media interviews and testified before several state legislatures.

Recently she said, "Stigma is no longer an issue. People now adopt from Russia and China. It isn't hush-hush anymore."

Her comments represent a common, recurring pattern. In Jean M. Paton's historic 1950's adoption study, 40 anonymous men and women adopted before 1932 broke their silence. A 30 year old participant says, "Nowadays, adoption is not frowned on...like it was in the 191-s" (Paton, 1954, p. 154). A 40 year old declares, "Making [adoptees] realize...that they do not bear any stigma because of the circumstances ... [of] ...their birth. There is more understanding of all these things now then there was even 10 years ago (Paton, 1954, p. 156)."

A 1998 Boston Globe headline suggests that adoption stigma is fading, though some sting remains.

In 2003, an Internet adoption expert referred to sealed records as the last remaining stigma.

Last spring Ontario's privacy commissioner said, "Lives would be 'shattered' if the province retroactively opens up sealed records and reveals the secrets of women who gave up children years ago." The 2005 anti-adoptee media campaign waged in Ontario against Bill 183 reached adopteephobic levels.

Last winter Nebraska's governor approved legislative bill 61. Now heirs 21 years or older of adopted persons may access their adopted ancestors' original birth certificates providing the adopted ancestors' birth parents and their spouses are deceased, and 100 years has passed since the adopted ancestors' birth.

Meanwhile, Reactive Attachment Disorder of Infancy and Early Childhood, (RAD) like Attention Deficit Disorder, (ADD) and Adopted Child Syndrome, (ACS) has become the latest adopted child diagnosis *de jour.*

Adoption and stigma continue to be inescapably intertwined. A prevailing cultural bias remains.   Its passive acceptance is the norm.

Joanne Wolf Small, 2006

181

About the Author

Though Joanne Wolf Small, M.S.W. had lived adoption for three decades, she knew next to nothing about it as a social institution. After completing a search for her birth family, co-organizing Adoptees In Search, obtaining a Masters in clinical social work, and serving on a Federal adoption advisory panel she found a major discrepancy between child welfare's idiosyncratic representation of adoption, and the experiences of adopted persons, and birth and adoptive parents that live it. Her belief in the adoptive family as a positive alternate is dissonant with a widespread and covertly held negative public image.

Her professional experience includes a post-adoption clinical practice, clinical supervision, in-service training, and seminars, lectures, publications, and interviews with over a thousand adoptive family members.

LaVergne, TN USA
12 December 2009

166819LV00006B/39/A